200 **more** slow cooker recipes

hamlyn **all color cookbook**

200 more slow cooker recipes

Sara Lewis

An Hachette UK Company
www.hachette.co.uk

First published in Great Britain in 2011 by
Hamlyn, a division of Octopus Publishing Group Ltd
Endeavour House
189 Shaftesbury Avenue
London
WC2H 8JY
www.octopusbooksusa.com

This edition published in 2011

Distributed in the U.S. and Canada by Octopus Books USA:
c/o Hachette Book Group
237 Park Avenue
New York, NY 10017

ISBN 978-0-600-62339-7

Printed and bound in China

10 9 8 7 6 5 4 3 2 1

Notes
Standard level spoon measures are used in all recipes

Medium eggs have been used throughout.

Fresh herbs should be used unless otherwise stated.

A few recipes contain nuts and nut derivatives. Anyone with a
known nut allergy must avoid these.

This book contains some dishes made with raw or lightly
cooked eggs. It is prudent for more vulnerable people such as
pregnant and nursing mothers, invalids, the elderly, babies,
and young children to avoid raw or lightly cooked eggs.

Read your slow cooker manual before you begin and
preheat the slow cooker if required according to the
manufacturer's instructions. Because slow cookers vary
slightly from manufacturer to manufacturer, check recipe
timings with the manufacturer's directions for a recipe
using the same ingredients.

All recipes for this book were tested in oval-shaped slow
cookers with a working capacity of 2½ quarts, total capacity of
3½ quarts using metric measurements. Where the slow cooker
recipe is finished off under the broiler, remove the pot from
the machine housing using oven mitts.

contents

introduction   6

soups   16

light bites & everyday suppers   50

short-cut suppers   90

vegetarian   120

food for friends   148

desserts   176

drinks & preserves   212

index   234

acknowledgments   240

introduction

introduction

It might seem a contradiction in terms but if you are short of time and cash a slow cooker could be the answer. Grabbing a cook-chill meal from the supermarket as you struggle to get home is not relaxing or cheap, especially when feeding a family. Adjusting the way you cook may solve the problem—trying to fit everything in at the end of the day when everyone is tired is not always the best solution.

Making supper first thing may sound odd, but why not come back and get supper on after dropping the kids at school in the morning or add things to the slow cooker pot before you even get dressed in your smart work clothes? Then, when you walk in the door later in the day, what could be more welcoming than the lovely aroma of supper ready and waiting. Or, if you feel you wouldn't be organized enough for this, get the slow cooker bubbling away on a Saturday morning so that you are free to do all those things you

want to—enjoy time with the family, get on with a DIY or gardening project, or spend a few hours at the gym.

Throughout this book there are recipes for all kind of occasions—from food to share with friends to everyday basics, warming soups for lunch to cheap, filling end-of-the-month suppers. While everyone knows that a slow cooker is great for cooking meaty casseroles, there are also light, fresh-tasting fish dishes or great recipes for those who would rather have a veggie option and even desserts, too, for those days when you need spoiling. There are recipes for hot punches and preserves—perhaps not the kind of slow cooker recipes that automatically spring to mind.

choosing a slow cooker

Slow cookers come in a range of sizes and shapes but the most versatile must be the midsized, oval-shaped slow cooker—it is large enough to pot roast a chicken or half shoulder of lamb, to make a meaty casserole or chili for four, a soup for six or a steamed pud, or four individual puds, for a weekend treat. When shopping, look for one that has a total capacity of 3½ quarts and a working capacity of 2½ quarts. All the recipes in this book have been tested in a slow cooker this size, but if you choose to buy a bigger or smaller cooker, simply halve the ingredients

or add half as much again where appropriate.

It is easy to get carried away and buy a large slow cooker on special offer. These may seem good value, but a slow cooker really needs to be half-full with food to work well, so if there are only four in your family do you really want to be cooking casseroles for six each time you use your slow cooker?

Recipes cooked in a pudding mold, individual dishes, or a soufflé-style dish can be cooked in the larger slow cooker in just the same way as the midsized slow cooker—there will just be more room for water around the dishes.

If you are a couple rather than a family you may prefer to buy the midsized slow cooker and freeze the extra two portions for another night. Also look out for the smaller two-portion-sized slow cookers with a maximum capacity of 1½ quarts and a working capacity of 1 quart.

Some of the more expensive models have slow cooker pots that can also be used on the stovetop to fry foods first, but if you

already have a good skillet this is not an essential requirement.

Choose a slow cooker with high and low settings and an indicator light so that you can see at a glance if the slow cooker is on before you leave the house. Nothing is more frustrating than coming home to find you forgot to turn the slow cooker on after all! Check the lid of the slow cooker, too, when buying—the best models have a lid without a steam vent.

what can I cook in it?

A slow cooker is surprisingly versatile. It is well known that it cooks savory casseroles well, but it is also great for steamed puds. Unlike simmering a mold in a steamer, where you need to regularly check the water levels in the bottom of the pan, a slow cooker is very unlikely to boil dry, so you can put the pudding on to cook and then practically forget about it. If cooking a large Sunday lunch or a big festive dinner it also means that you can free up an extra burner on the stove, which can be invaluable. As with all slow cooker recipes, if you get a little delayed the pudding will not spoil. However old fashioned steamed puddings may be, they are very often made with pantry ingredients meaning one can be rustled up without a special shopping trip or at great expense.

For something a little lighter, try a warm chocolate mousse dessert or delicate baked custard, crème brûlée or crème caramel, even a baked cheesecake. Baked apples are very successful, as are fresh and fruity compotes, which are delicious with yogurt or ice cream.

Using the slow cooker as a water bath also means that you can bake savory dishes, too, such as a baked egg tortilla or frittata. Pâtés and terrines can also be made, while slow-cooked duck rillettes—a French version of potted meat—are particularly successful, cooked directly in the slow cooker pot.

Although meaty casseroles are great, fish recipes also work very well. The gentle heat means that the fish stays moist and doesn't break into pieces during cooking. Try mackerel, trout, a large piece of salmon or individual portions. Shellfish can be added, but do so at the end of cooking and make sure that shrimp, squid, or mussels are thoroughly defrosted if frozen. Cook on high for the last 20–30 minutes of cooking. Seafood is delicious added to garlicky tomato sauce for an easy pasta topper.

Rice-based dishes can be slow cooked, although for best results use easy-cook rice that has been partially cooked first so it is less starchy and so less sticky. If using basmati rice, rinse it in plenty of cold water to remove some of the starch before cooking. When cooking rice, allow a minimum of 1 cup water for each ½ cup easy-cook rice, or up to 2 cups water for the same quantity of risotto rice. When making a risotto in the slow cooker, add the hot stock all in one go and adjust with a little extra hot stock at the end if needed. For rice pudding, make with risotto rice, too, as it cooks more quickly than traditional round-grain white pudding rice.

For those who would rather eat less meat or no meat at all, suppers can be based around lentils, pearl barley, and canned beans, which can be added straight to the slow cooker. Dried beans and split peas need soaking in cold water overnight, then boiling rapidly in water for 10 minutes before draining and cooking in the slow cooker.

slow cooker basics

- Some slow cookers require preheating, others do not; always check the manufacturer's instructions before you begin.
- If cooking food in a mold, individual dishes, or a soufflé-style dish, make sure these will fit in your slow cooker pot before you begin making the recipe.
- Foods cooked in a slow cooker must contain liquid; to ensure even cooking press meat, fish, or vegetables below the surface of the liquid.

- Foods will not brown in a slow cooker, so fry foods before they go in or brown the top by transferring the slow cooker pot from its housing to the broiler just before serving. Alternatively use a kitchen torch.
- The smaller the pieces of food, the quicker they will cook.
- Food at the bottom of the slow cooker pot will cook more quickly so put root vegetables into the pot first.
- Don't worry if you get delayed, the food will be fine for an extra hour or so.

do I have to cook things first?

No—meat, fish, vegetables, and lentils and grains that don't require soaking first can be put straight into the slow cooker pot but crucially they must then be covered with hot stock or liquid. This saves time and saves you standing over the cooker in your smart work suit before rushing out in the morning. Prepare as much of the recipe as you can the night before—chop or slice onions, cube meat, mix flavorings together and then cover and chill in the refrigerator. However, don't be tempted to part-fry meat the night before and then add cold to the slow cooker the day after.

Pour stock or sauce ingredients into a saucepan and bring to a boil on the stovetop or microwave in a bowl, then pour into the slow cooker and cover and cook. Allow an extra hour or two onto the recipe to make sure that the meat is really tender.

Although not essential, if you have the time, fry the meat first for the best flavor and color, just as you would if preparing a dish to go into the oven.

how full should the pot be?

A slow cooker is really like a large insulated saucepan and although it must never be used without liquid the amount needed is less than when you are simmering a pan on the stovetop as there is no danger that a slow cooker will boil dry. As the stew or casserole heats up, the liquid turns to steam, which condenses on the lid and falls back into the pot.

Aim to fill the slow cooker pot between half and three-quarters full. Joints of meat should fill the pot no more than two-thirds full. If you are using a pudding mold allow ½ inch at the narrowest point in an oval pot or ¾ inch in a round one and then pour hot water into the gap between the mold and the pot so that it comes halfway up the sides. If you are making soup the pot can be a little fuller, but make sure the liquid level is no higher than 1 inch from the top.

what setting is best?

Most slow cookers come with two settings—high and low—while others may also have an auto setting or medium or warm setting for greater flexibility. In general, the high setting will take half the time of the low setting. Both settings will reach just below 212°F, or boiling point, during cooking, but when set to high the temperature is reached more quickly.

An auto setting is not vital but it is helpful if you plan to add meat without frying it first as it will automatically start the slow cooker on high, then reduce to low by means of a thermostat. If your slow cooker doesn't have this then set to high for 30 minutes and then reduce to low manually.

Increasing the temperature from low to high at the end of cooking can also be useful if you want to thicken the casserole with cornstarch, add green vegetables, shellfish, or dumplings. The warm setting can be used after the cooking time is finished so is ideal for those who want to serve supper in two sittings.

how do you work out timings?

- Most casserole-style dishes made with diced meat, ground meat, or chicken leg joints are cooked on low for 8–10 hours.
- Larger items such as joints of meat, pot roasts, turkey drumsticks, lamb shanks, and meaty terrines are cooked on high for 5–7 hours.
- Soups are cooked on low for 6–8 hours.
- Egg-style tortillas and frittatas are cooked on low for 2–2½ hours, individual baked eggs on high for 40–50 minutes.
- Baked fish is cooked on low for 1½–2 hours, fish pie on low for 2–3 hours, fish terrine on high for 3–4 hours.
- Rice dishes are cooked on low for 1¾–2 hours.
- Large steamed puds are cooked on high for 4–5 hours, individual ones on high for 2–3 hours.

adjusting the cooking time

If you want to slow down or speed up the timings for diced meat or vegetable casseroles, adjust the heat settings and timings as suggested below:

Low	Medium	High
6–8 hours	4–6 hours	3–4 hours
8–10 hours	6–8 hours	5–6 hours
10–12 hours	8–10 hours	7–8 hours

These timings were taken from the Morphy Richards slow cooker instruction handbook. Do not change timings or settings for fish, whole joints, or dairy dishes in recipes.

there seems to be a lot of water around the lid, is this ok?

Yes perfectly—as the slow cooker comes up to temperature the steam condenses and forms a seal around the lid. Every time you lift the lid you break the seal and add an extra 20 minutes to the cooking time. Resist the temptation to lift the lid more than is absolutely necessary. It takes the slow cooker 1 hour to come up to a safe and optimal temperature.

how will I know if the food is ready and cooked through?

This is particularly crucial when cooking meat and fish, but especially when cooking joints. Test as you would if cooking in a conventional

oven by inserting a knife into the center, or through the thickest part of the leg into the breast if testing a whole chicken. The juices that run out should be clear with no hint of pink and the tip of the knife should feel hot. The knife will also slide into meat easily if tender. For smaller chunks or cubes of meat, take a piece out, cut in half and if done, taste for tenderness. Diced casseroled beef will take considerably longer to cook if it is not fried first.

When testing chicken or duck portions or lamb shanks, the meat will begin to shrink away from the bone when tender; as with the larger joints, press a knife into the thickest part of the joint.

For extra piece of mind a digital meat probe can be a fail-safe way to check as it will tell you exactly the internal temperature of the meat; it can also be used when roasting meat in a traditional oven and some types can be used when making jam, boiling sugar, or deep-frying on the stovetop.

Fish should break easily into even-colored flakes when pressed in the center with a knife.

can I use my own recipes?

Of course—to get an idea of timings and amounts that will fit in your slow cooker pot, look up a recipe in the following pages with the same main ingredient and use the amount of liquid suggested in that recipe as a starting point. As a slow cooker uses such gentle heat you will find that you do not need quite

13

the same amount of liquid as you would if making a stovetop stew as there is no danger of a slow cooker drying out.

Nearly all meaty or vegetable stews, casseroles, slow cook curries, or chili can be cooked successfully in the slow cooker; so too can steamed puddings, custards, and terrines.

Root vegetables take a surprisingly long time to cook and can take longer to cook than diced beef, especially if the beef has been fried off first. The secret is to cut the vegetables the same size or a little smaller than the meat so that it will all be cooked at the same time, and, if using a mix of different root veggies, to cut them all to a similar size so that they will all be ready at the same time. As the heating elements are in the base and around the sides of the slow cooker, put the vegetables into the slow cooker pot where it will be hottest.

If using a high proportion of fresh tomatoes mixed with stock, reduce the liquid level by one-third or even half, as the tomatoes will give off a lot of juice as they cook down.

If using the slow cooker to steam puddings or to use as a water bath for baked custards or terrines, check that the dish you are going to use will fit into the slow cooker before you begin. You may not be able to fit four standard-sized ramekin dishes into every type of slow cooker, but generally individual dishes that have slightly sloping sides will fit in fine; look out for individual ¾ cup metal pudding molds in your local cook store or try with heatproof tea cups or mugs.

short of time?

Cheat—use a few short cuts such as ready-made cans or jars of sauce—even a can of tomato, chicken, or spiced soup can be used as a speedy cook-in-sauce poured over some fried onions, fried chicken pieces, or sausages. If you are really short of time then don't fry the meat first—this works best with diced lamb or boneless chicken thighs or ready-made meatballs. Make sure to bring the liquid up to a boil in a saucepan on the stovetop or in a bowl in the microwave before adding. Add everything to the slow cooker pot and cook on high for at least 30 minutes before reducing to low when you go out.

Bought sauces tend to be quite highly seasoned so taste at the end of cooking and adjust with extra salt and pepper just before serving, if needed.

caring for your slow cooker

Because a slow cooker heats food to a lower heat than a conventional oven there are no burnt-on splashes or stubborn marks to get rid of. At the end of cooking, remove the empty earthenware pot from the slow cooker, fill it with warm soapy water and allow to soak, if necessary, then remove any marks with a dish brush. Don't stand the pot in water—the unglazed areas are porous and so will soak up water and could then possibly crack when heated in the slow cooker. Some pots are dishwasher safe, but not all, so check with your instruction handbook first.

Wipe out the inside of the slow cooker machine with a damp cloth and a squirt of cream cleanser, making sure that it is unplugged first. Buff up the outside with a dry cloth. Never immerse in water.

safety tips

• Always read the instruction handbook that accompanies your slow cooker before you begin.
• Make sure frozen food is completely defrosted before adding to the slow cooker, with the exception of a small quantity of frozen peas or corn toward the end of cooking, or frozen fruit.
• Add hot liquid or stock to the slow cooker pot; this is especially important if the meat is not fried first.
• Don't lift the lid off the slow cooker during the first hour of cooking while the slow

cooker heats up to a safe and optimal temperature.
• Lift dishes out of the slow cooker pot using a dish towel or use foil straps (see below).
• The outside of the slow cooker housing gets hot when in use—use oven mitts if removing the pot from the housing as soon as cooking has finished.
• Never reheat already cooked food in a slow cooker.
• Don't leave cooked food to cool down in the turned-off slow cooker.

removing a pudding mold from the slow cooker

So that you can easily lift a hot mold out of the slow cooker, tear off two long pieces of foil. Fold each into thirds to make a long, thin strap. Put one on top of the other to make a cross, then sit the pudding mold in the center. Lift up the straps, then lower the basin into the slow cooker pot carefully. Use the straps to remove the basin at the end of cooking.

soups

vegetable broth with dumplings

Preparation time **35 minutes**
Cooking temperature **low**
Cooking time **8¾–11 hours**
Serves **4**

3 tablespoons **butter**
1 **leek**, sliced; white and
   green parts kept separate
1 cup diced **rutabaga**
1 cup diced **parsnips**
1 cup diced **carrots**
1 **celery stick**, sliced
¼ cup **pearl barley**
4 cups boiling **vegetable** or
   chicken stock
2–3 sprigs of **sage**
1 teaspoon **English mustard**
salt and **pepper**

Dumplings
¾ cup **self-rising flour**
⅓ cup **vegetable suet**
2 **bacon slices**, finely diced
about 3 tablespoons **water**

Preheat the slow cooker if necessary; see the manufacturer's instructions. Heat the butter in a large skillet, add the white leek slices and fry for 2–3 minutes until softened. Stir in the root vegetables and celery and fry for 4–5 minutes.

Add the pearl barley to the slow cooker pot. Then add the fried vegetables, boiling stock, and sage. Stir in the mustard and a little salt and pepper. Cover with the lid and cook on low for 8–10 hours or until the vegetables and barley are tender.

Make the dumplings. Put the flour, suet, bacon, and a little salt and pepper in a bowl and mix well. Gradually stir in enough water to make a soft but not sticky dough. Knead lightly on a floured surface, then shape into 12 balls.

Stir the reserved green leek slices into the soup, add the dumplings, spacing them slightly apart, then replace the lid and cook, still on low, for 45–60 minutes or until light and fluffy. Ladle into bowls and serve.

For chicken broth with mini herb dumplings, fry 4 small chicken thighs on the bone with the white leek slices. Add the root vegetables and celery, omitting the parsnips. Continue and cook as above for 8–10 hours. Make the dumplings with 2 tablespoons mixed chopped parsley or chives and sage instead of the bacon. Lift the chicken out of the soup, discard the skin and bones and chop the meat into small pieces. Return the meat to the pot with the raw dumplings and green leeks and cook for 45–60 minutes.

mulligatawny soup

Preparation time **15 minutes**
Cooking temperature **low**
Cooking time **6–8 hours**
Serves **4–6**

1 **onion**, chopped
1 **carrot**, diced
1 **dessert apple**, cored and
   coarsely grated
2 **garlic cloves**, finely
   chopped
13 oz can **chopped tomatoes**
⅓ cup **red lentils**
⅓ cup **golden raisins**
3 teaspoons **mild curry paste**
5 cups boiling **vegetable** or
   chicken stock
salt and **pepper**

Croutes
¼ cup **butter**
2 **garlic cloves**, finely
   chopped
3 tablespoons chopped
   cilantro
8–12 slices of **French-style**
   bread, depending on size

Preheat the slow cooker if necessary; see the manufacturer's instructions. Put the vegetables, apple, garlic, tomatoes, lentils, and golden raisins into the slow cooker pot.

Add the curry paste, then stir in the boiling stock and add a little salt and pepper. Cover and cook on low for 6–8 hours or until the lentils are soft and the carrots are tender.

When almost ready to serve, make the croutes. Beat together the butter, garlic, and chopped cilantro in a bowl. Toast the bread on both sides, then spread with the butter. Ladle the soup into shallow bowls and serve topped with the croutes.

For gingered carrot soup, put 3 cups diced carrots and 1½ inches peeled and finely chopped fresh ginger root into the slow cooker pot with the onion, lentils and curry paste, omitting the other ingredients. Pour over 5 cups boiling vegetable stock and continue as above. Puree with an immersion blender, mix in 1¼ cups milk, and cook on high for 15 minutes until piping hot. Ladle into bowls and serve with swirls of plain yogurt.

old english pea & ham soup

Preparation time **15 minutes**
Cooking temperature **high**
Cooking time **5–6 hours**
Serves **4–6**

¾ cup dried **green split peas**,
   soaked overnight in cold
   water
2 **onions**, chopped
2 **celery sticks**, diced
1 **carrot**, diced
6 cups **water**
3 teaspoons **English mustard**
1 **bay leaf**
small **unsmoked boneless
   ham joint**, about 1 lb
4 tablespoons chopped
   parsley
salt and **pepper**

Preheat the slow cooker if necessary; see the
manufacturer's instructions. Drain the peas and add
to a large saucepan with the onions, celery, carrot,
and water. Bring to a boil, skim if needed, and boil
for 10 minutes.

Pour the mixture into the slow cooker pot, then stir in
the mustard, bay leaf, and some black pepper. Rinse the
ham joint in several changes of cold water, then add to
the pot and press below the surface of the liquid. Cover
and cook on high for 5–6 hours or until the peas are
soft and the ham cooked through.

Lift the ham joint out of the slow cooker pot with a
carving fork, drain well, then cut away the zest and
fat. Cut the meat into bite-size pieces. Puree the soup
with an immersion blender or leave chunky, if preferred.
Stir the ham back into the pot and mix in the parsley.
Taste and adjust the seasoning, adding salt, if needed.
Ladle the soup into bowls and serve with crusty bread.

For split pea & parsnip soup, soak ¾ cup yellow split
peas as above. Drain and put into a saucepan with
1 chopped onion, 2 cups diced parsnips, and 6 cups
chicken or vegetable stock. Boil for 10 minutes, then
transfer to the slow cooker pot. Cover and cook as
above. Puree and adjust the seasoning, if needed.
Beat ⅛ cup butter with 2 finely chopped garlic cloves,
3 tablespoons chopped cilantro, 1 teaspoon roughly
crushed cumin seeds, and 1 teaspoon roughly crushed
cilantro seeds. Ladle the soup into bowls and top with
spoonfuls of the butter.

chicken & tortelloni soup

Preparation time **15 minutes**
Cooking temperature **high**
Cooking time **5¼–7½ hours**
Serves **4**

1 **chicken carcass**
1 **onion**, quartered
2 **celery sticks**, sliced
2 **carrots**, thinly sliced
2 sprigs of **thyme** or **basil**
5 cups boiling **water**
½ teaspoon **black
  peppercorns**, roughly
  crushed
salt
3 cups **spinach**, washed,
  drained and
  roughly torn
3 **tomatoes**, diced
8 oz fresh **spinach tortelloni**
freshly grated **Parmesan
  cheese**, to serve

Preheat the slow cooker if necessary; see the manufacturer's instructions. Put the chicken carcass into the slow cooker pot, breaking it in half if needed. Add the vegetables, herbs, and boiling water, then add the peppercorns and salt.

Cover with the lid and cook on high for 5–7 hours. Lift the carcass out of the slow cooker pot and remove any meat; cut this into small pieces and reserve. Strain the stock, discarding the bones, vegetables, and herbs, then pour the hot stock back into the slow cooker pot.

Add the shredded chicken, spinach, tomatoes, and tortelloni. Replace the lid and cook for 20–30 minutes, still on high, until piping hot. Ladle the soup into bowls and serve sprinkled with a little grated Parmesan.

For pesto & lemon soup, cook the chicken carcass as above, then stir 2 teaspoons pesto sauce and the grated zest and juice of 1 lemon into the strained stock. Mix in ¾ cup finely chopped broccoli, 1 cup frozen peas, and 4 cups roughly chopped spinach with the shredded chicken, omitting the tomatoes and tortelloni. Cook as above and serve topped with extra pesto and grated Parmesan.

haddock & bacon chowder

Preparation time **15 minutes**
Cooking temperature **high**
Cooking time **2½–3½ hours**
Serves **4**

2 tablespoons **butter**
1 **onion**, finely chopped
10 oz **potatoes**, cut into
  small dice
4 **bacon slices**, diced
3 cups boiling **fish stock**
1 cup frozen **corn kernels**,
  thawed
1 **bay leaf**
1 lb **smoked haddock**,
  skinned
⅔ cup **heavy cream**
salt and **pepper**
chopped **parsley**, to garnish

Preheat the slow cooker if necessary; see the
manufacturer's instructions. Heat the butter in a large
skillet, add the onion, potatoes, and bacon and fry
gently, stirring, until just beginning to brown.

Transfer the potato mixture to the slow cooker pot.
Pour over the boiling stock, then add the corn, bay leaf,
and a little salt and pepper. Cover with the lid and cook
on high for 2–3 hours or until the potatoes are tender.

Add the fish and press it just below the surface of the
stock, cutting the pieces in half, if needed. Replace
the lid and cook, still on high, for 30 minutes or until
the fish flakes easily when pressed in the center with
a knife.

Lift the fish onto a plate with a spatula and break it
into flakes with a knife and fork, checking for and
removing any bones. Stir the cream into the soup, then
return the fish. Ladle the soup into bowls and sprinkle
with parsley.

For salmon & crab chowder, fry the onion and
potatoes, omitting the bacon, and continue and cook
for 2–3 hours as above. Replace the smoked haddock
with a 1¾ oz can dressed brown crabmeat, stirred
into the potato mixture, and 1 lb salmon fillet, cut into
4 strips and pressed below the surface of the stock.
Cook for 30–40 minutes until salmon is cooked, then
continue as above.

thai coconut & butternut soup

Preparation time **20 minutes**
Cooking temperature **low**
Cooking time **7–8 hours**
Serves **4–6**

1 tablespoon **sunflower oil**
1 **onion**, chopped
4 teaspoons **Thai red curry paste**
1 teaspoon **galangal paste**
2 **garlic cloves**, finely chopped
1 **butternut squash**, about 2 lb, peeled, seeded, and cut into ¾ inch chunks
1 cup **coconut cream**
3 cups **vegetable stock**
1 tablespoon **soy sauce**
small bunch of **cilantro**
salt and **pepper**

Preheat the slow cooker if necessary; see the manufacturer's instructions. Heat the oil in a large skillet, add the onion, and fry until softened. Stir in the curry paste, galangal, and garlic and cook for 1 minute, then mix in the squash.

Pour in the coconut cream and stock, then add the soy sauce and bring to a boil, stirring. Pour into the slow cooker pot, cover with the lid, and cook on low for 7–8 hours or until the squash is tender. (You may find that the coconut cream separates slightly but this will disappear after pureeing.)

Puree the soup while still in the slow cooker pot with an immersion blender. Alternatively, transfer to a blender and puree, in batches if necessary, until smooth, then return it to the slow cooker pot and reheat on high for 15 minutes.

Reserve a few sprigs of cilantro for garnish, chop the rest, and stir into the soup. Ladle the soup into bowls and garnish with the reserved cilantro sprigs.

For butternut & orange soup, fry the onion in 2 tablespoons butter, then add the diced butternut squash with the grated zest and juice of 2 small oranges, 3¾ cups vegetable stock, and 3 whole star anise. Bring to a boil, stirring, add a little salt and pepper and continue as above. Remove the star anise before pureeing and serve with swirls of cream.

tomato & red pepper soup

Preparation time **15 minutes**
Cooking temperature **high**
Cooking time **2½–3 hours**
Serves **4–6**

2 tablespoons **olive oil**
1 **onion**, chopped
1 **red bell pepper**, cored,
  seeded, and diced
1½ lb **tomatoes**, roughly
  chopped
1 **garlic clove**, finely chopped
2½ cups **vegetable stock**
1 tablespoon **tomato paste**
2 teaspoons **superfine sugar**
1 tablespoon **balsamic
  vinegar**, plus extra to garnish
salt and **pepper**

Preheat the slow cooker if necessary; see the manufacturer's instructions. Heat the oil in a large skillet, add the onion, and fry until softened. Stir in the red pepper, tomatoes, and garlic and fry for 1–2 minutes.

Pour in the stock and add the tomato paste, sugar, vinegar, and a little salt and pepper and bring to a boil, stirring. Pour into the slow cooker pot, cover with the lid, and cook on high for 2½–3 hours or until the vegetables are tender.

Puree the soup while still in the slow cooker pot with an immersion blender. Alternatively, transfer to a blender and puree, in batches if necessary, until smooth, then return to the slow cooker pot and reheat on high for 15 minutes.

Taste and adjust the seasoning, if needed, then ladle the soup into bowls and garnish with a drizzle of extra vinegar or stir in spoonfuls of scallion pesto (see below).

For scallion & basil pesto to garnish the soup, roughly chop 4 scallions, then finely chop with an immersion blender in a bowl, or in a blender, with 4 sprigs of basil, ¼ cup freshly grated Parmesan cheese, 4 tablespoons olive oil, and a little pepper until a coarse paste. Spoon over the top of the soup just before serving.

lamb & barley broth

Preparation time **15 minutes**
Cooking temperature **low**
Cooking time **8–10 hours**
Serves **4–6**

2 tablespoons **butter**
1 tablespoon **sunflower oil**
1 **lamb leg chop** or 4 oz
   boned rib of lamb, diced
1 **onion**, chopped
1 small **leek**, chopped
3 cups mixed **parsnip,
   rutabaga**, **turnip**, and
   carrot, cut into small dice
¼ cup **pearl barley**
5 cups **lamb** or **chicken stock**
¼ teaspoon **ground allspice**
2–3 sprigs of **rosemary**
salt and **pepper**
chopped **parsley** or **chives**, to
   garnish (optional)

Preheat the slow cooker if necessary; see the manufacturer's instructions. Heat the butter and oil in a large skillet, add the lamb, onion, and leek and fry, stirring, until the lamb is lightly browned.

Stir in the root vegetables and barley, then add the stock, allspice, rosemary, and plenty of salt and pepper and bring to a boil, stirring. Pour into the slow cooker pot, cover with the lid, and cook on low for 8–10 hours or until the barley is tender.

Stir well, taste, and adjust the seasoning, if needed, then ladle the soup into bowls. Garnish with chopped herbs, if desired, and serve with warm bread.

For Hungarian chorba, fry the lamb and vegetables as above, omitting the pearl barley. Stir in 1 teaspoon smoked paprika, then add ¼ cup long-grain rice and a few sprigs of dill weed. Stir in 5 cups lamb stock, 2 tablespoons red wine vinegar, and 1 tablespoon light brown sugar. Add salt and pepper, bring to a boil, and continue as above. Garnish with extra chopped dill and serve with rye bread.

carrot & cumin soup

Preparation time **20 minutes**
Cooking temperature **low**
Cooking time **7–8 hours**
Serves **4–6**

1 tablespoon **sunflower oil**
1 large **onion**, chopped
1¼ lb **carrots**, thinly sliced
1½ teaspoons **cumin seeds**,
  roughly crushed
1 teaspoon **turmeric**
¼ cup **long-grain rice**
5 cups **vegetable stock**
salt and **pepper**

To serve
⅔ cup **natural yogurt**
mango chutney
a few **pappadams**

Preheat the slow cooker if necessary; see the manufacturer's instructions. Heat the oil in a large skillet, add the onion, and fry over a medium heat, stirring, until softened. Stir in the carrots, cumin seeds, and turmeric and fry for 2–3 minutes to release the cumin flavor and brown the onions.

Stir in the rice, then add the stock and a little salt and pepper and bring to a boil. Pour into the slow cooker pot, cover with the lid, and cook on low for 7–8 hours or until the carrots are tender.

Puree the soup while still in the slow cooker pot with an immersion blender. Alternatively, transfer to a blender and puree, in batches if necessary, until smooth, then return to the slow cooker pot and reheat on high for 15 minutes.

Taste and adjust the seasoning, if needed, then ladle the soup into bowls. Top with spoonfuls of yogurt and a little mango chutney and serve with pappadams.

For spiced parsnip soup, fry the onion as above, replacing the carrots with 1¼ lb halved and thinly sliced parsnips and adding 1 teaspoon turmeric, 1 teaspoon ground cumin, 1 teaspoon ground coriander, and 1½ inches peeled and finely chopped fresh ginger root. Continue as above.

minestrone soup

Preparation time **15 minutes**
Cooking temperature **low** and
 high
Cooking time **6¼–8½ hours**
Serves **4**

1 tablespoon **olive oil**
1 **onion**, chopped
1 **carrot**, diced
2 **bacon slices**, diced
2 **garlic cloves**, finely
 chopped
4 **tomatoes**, skinned and
 chopped
2 **celery sticks**, diced
2 small **zucchini**, diced
3 teaspoons **pesto**, plus extra
 to serve
5 cups **chicken** or **vegetable
 stock**
3 oz **purple sprouting
 broccoli**, stems and florets
 cut into small pieces
3 tablespoons tiny **soup
 pasta**
salt and **pepper**
freshly grated **Parmesan
 cheese**, to serve

Preheat the slow cooker if necessary; see the
manufacturer's instructions. Heat the oil in a large
skillet, add the onion, carrot, and bacon and fry, stirring,
until lightly browned.

Add the garlic, then stir in the tomatoes, celery, and
zucchini and cook for 1–2 minutes. Stir in the pesto
and stock, then add a little salt and pepper and bring
to a boil, stirring.

Pour into the slow cooker pot, cover with the lid, and
cook on low for 6–8 hours or until the vegetables are
tender. Add the broccoli and pasta, replace the lid,
and cook on high for 15–30 minutes or until the
pasta is tender.

Stir well, taste, and adjust the seasoning, if needed,
then ladle the soup into bowls. Top with extra spoonfuls
of pesto, to taste, and sprinkle with grated Parmesan.
Serve with crusty bread.

For curried vegetable & chicken soup, omit the
bacon and add the diced meat from 2 chicken
thighs when frying the onion and carrot. Add the
garlic, tomatoes, celery, and zucchini, then add
3 teaspoons mild curry paste instead of the pesto
and 3 tablespoons basmati rice. Add 5 cups chicken
stock and continue as above, omitting the pasta.
Garnish with chopped cilantro and serve with
warmed naan breads.

leek, potato, & stilton soup

Preparation time **25 minutes**
Cooking temperature **low**
Cooking time **5½–6½ hours**
Serves 4–6

2 tablespoons **butter**
1 tablespoon **sunflower oil**
1 lb **leeks**, thinly sliced; white
  and green parts kept
  separate
1 **Canadian bacon slice**,
  diced, plus 4 broiled **slices**,
  chopped, to garnish
12 oz **potatoes**, diced
3¾ cups **chicken** or **vegetable**
  stock
1¼ cups **milk**
⅔ cup **heavy cream**
5 oz **mature Stilton cheese**
  (rind removed), diced
salt and **pepper**

Preheat the slow cooker if necessary; see the manufacturer's instructions. Heat the butter and oil in a large skillet, then add the white leek slices, the diced bacon and potatoes and fry over a medium heat, stirring, until just beginning to turn golden.

Pour in the stock, add a little salt and pepper, and bring to a boil, stirring. Transfer to the slow cooker pot, cover with the lid, and cook on low for 5–6 hours. Stir the reserved green leek slices and milk into the slow cooker pot. Replace the lid and cook, still on low, for 30 minutes or until the leeks are tender. Roughly puree the soup in the pot with an immersion blender or use a masher, if preferred.

Mix in the cream and two-thirds of the cheese and continue stirring until the cheese has melted. Taste and adjust the seasoning, if needed, then ladle the soup into bowls and sprinkle with the remaining cheese and chopped broiled bacon.

For cock-a-leekie soup, heat the butter and oil as above, then add 2 chicken thighs on the bone and fry until golden, remove them from pan and put into the slow cooker pot. Fry the leeks, bacon, and potatoes as above, then mix in 5 cups chicken stock, ⅓ cup pitted prunes, chopped, and a sprig of thyme. Season, bring to a boil, then transfer to the pot. Cover and cook on low for 8–10 hours. Take the chicken off the bone, discarding the skin, then dice the meat and return it to the pot with the green leek slices. Cook for 30 minutes, then ladle into bowls. Omit the milk, cream, Stilton, and bacon garnish.

crab gumbo

Preparation time **15 minutes**
Cooking temperature **high**
Cooking time **3¼–4½ hours**
Serves **4**

1 tablespoon **sunflower oil**
1 **onion**, finely chopped
1 **garlic clove**, chopped
2 **celery sticks**, sliced
1 **carrot**, cut into small dice
13 oz can **chopped tomatoes**
2½ cups **fish stock**
¼ cup easy-cook **long-grain rice**
1 **bay leaf**
2 sprigs of **thyme**
¼ teaspoon **dried red pepper flakes**
1 cup **okra**, sliced
1¾ oz can **dressed brown crabmeat**
salt and **pepper**
5¾ oz can **white crabmeat**, to serve (optional)

Preheat the slow cooker if necessary; see the manufacturer's instructions. Heat the oil in a large skillet, add the onion, and fry for 5 minutes or until softened.

Stir in the garlic, celery, and carrot, then mix in the tomatoes, stock, rice, herbs, and pepper flakes. Add a little salt and pepper and bring to a boil. Pour into the slow cooker pot, cover with the lid, and cook on high for 3–4 hours or until the vegetables and rice are tender.

Stir the soup, then add the okra and dressed brown crabmeat. Replace the lid and cook, still on high, for 20–30 minutes. Ladle the soup into bowls, top with the flaked white crabmeat, if desired, and serve with warm crusty bread.

For mixed vegetable gumbo, make up the soup as above, omitting the cans of brown and white crabmeat. Garnish with croutons made by frying 2 slices of bread, cut into cubes, in 2 tablespoons butter, 3 tablespoons olive oil, and ¼ teaspoon dried red pepper flakes until golden.

caramelized onion soup

Preparation time **25 minutes**
Cooking temperature **low**
Cooking time **4–5 hours**
Serves **4**

2 tablespoons **butter**
2 tablespoons **olive oil**
1 lb **onions**, thinly sliced
1 tablespoon **superfine sugar**
2 tablespoons **all-purpose flour**
1 cup **English beer**
3 cups **beef stock**
2 **bay leaves**
1 tablespoon **Worcestershire sauce**
salt and **pepper**

Cheesy croutes
8 slices of **French bread**
¾ cup grated **sharp cheddar cheese**
2 teaspoons **Worcestershire sauce**

Preheat the slow cooker if necessary; see the manufacturer's instructions. Heat the butter and oil in a large skillet, add the onions, and fry over a medium heat, stirring occasionally, for 15 minutes or until softened and just beginning to turn golden. Stir in the sugar and fry for 10 minutes, stirring frequently as the onions begin to caramelize and turn a deep golden brown.

Stir in the flour, then add the beer, stock, bay leaves, and Worcestershire sauce. Add a little salt and pepper and bring to a boil, stirring. Pour into the slow cooker pot, cover with the lid, and cook on low for 4–5 hours or until the onions are very soft.

When almost ready to serve, toast the French bread slices on both sides, sprinkle with the cheese and drizzle with the Worcestershire sauce. Broil until the cheese is bubbling. Ladle the soup into shallow bowls and float the croutes on top.

For French onion soup, fry the onions as above and stir in the flour. Replace the beer with 1 cup red wine and add with the stock, bay leaves, and salt and pepper, omitting the Worcestershire sauce. Continue as above. For the croutes, toast the French bread, then rub one side of each piece with a cut garlic clove and sprinkle with ¾ cup grated Gruyère cheese and broil. Serve as above.

tomato, lentil, & eggplant soup

Preparation time **20 minutes**
Cooking temperature **low**
Cooking time **6–8 hours**
Serves **4**

4 tablespoons **olive oil**, plus
  extra to garnish (optional)
1 **eggplant**, sliced
1 **onion**, chopped
2 **garlic cloves**, finely
  chopped
½ teaspoon **smoked paprika**
1 teaspoon **ground cumin**
½ cup **red lentils**
13 oz can **chopped tomatoes**
3 cups boiling **vegetable
  stock**
salt and **pepper**
chopped **cilantro**, to garnish

Preheat the slow cooker if necessary; see the
manufacturer's instructions. Heat 1 tablespoon of the
oil in a large skillet, add one-third of the eggplants and
fry on both sides until softened and golden. Scoop out
of the pan with a slotted spoon and transfer to a plate.
Repeat with the rest of the eggplants using 2 more
tablespoons of oil.

Add the remaining oil to the pan and fry the onion for
5 minutes or until softened. Stir in the garlic, paprika,
and cumin and cook for 1 minute, then mix in the lentils
and tomatoes. Add a little salt and pepper and bring to
a boil. Pour the mixture into the slow cooker pot and
stir in the boiling stock.

Cover with the lid and cook on low for 6–8 hours.
Serve the soup as it is or puree it with an immersion
blender, if preferred. Ladle the soup into bowls, drizzle
with a little extra olive oil, and sprinkle with cilantro.
Serve with toasted ciabatta bread.

For tomato, lentil, & chorizo soup, omit the eggplant
and fry the onion in 1 tablespoon olive oil. Add the
garlic, paprika, and ground cumin, then stir in 1 cored,
seeded, and diced red bell pepper and 2 oz diced
chorizo and fry for 2 minutes. Continue as above.

thai broth with fish dumplings

Preparation time **30 minutes**
Cooking temperature **low and high**
Cooking time **2¼–3¼ hours**
Serves **4**

3¾ cups boiling **fish stock**
2 teaspoons **Thai fish sauce** (nam pla)
1 tablespoon **Thai red curry paste**
1 tablespoon **soy sauce**
1 **carrot**, thinly sliced
2 **garlic cloves**, finely chopped
1 bunch of **asparagus**, trimmed and stems cut into 4
2 **bok choy**, thickly sliced

Dumplings
1 bunch of **scallions**, sliced
¾ cup **cilantro leaves**
1½ inches **fresh ginger root**, peeled and sliced
13 oz **cod**, skinned
1 tablespoon **cornstarch**
1 **egg white**

Preheat the slow cooker if necessary; see the manufacturer's instructions. Make the dumplings. Put half of the scallions into a food processor with the cilantro and ginger and chop finely. Add the cod, cornstarch and egg white and process until the fish is finely chopped. With wetted hands, shape the mixture into 12 balls.

Pour the boiling fish stock into the slow cooker pot, add the fish sauce, curry paste, and soy sauce. Add the rest of the scallions, the carrot, and garlic and drop in the dumplings. Cover with the lid and cook on low for 2–3 hours.

When almost ready to serve, add the asparagus and bok choy to the broth. Replace the lid and cook on high for 15 minutes or until just tender. Ladle into bowls and serve.

For Thai broth with noodles & shrimp, prepare and cook the broth as above, omitting the dumplings, for 2–3 hours. Add the asparagus, bok choy, and 7 oz frozen large shrimp, thoroughly thawed, and cook for 15 minutes on high. Meanwhile, soak 3 oz rice noodles in boiling water according to the package instructions. Drain and add to the bottom of 4 soup bowls. Ladle the broth on top and sprinkle with a little chopped cilantro.

cheesy cauliflower soup

Preparation time **20 minutes**
Cooking temperature **low** and **high**
Cooking time **4¼–5¼ hours**
Serves **4**

2 tablespoons **butter**
1 tablespoon **olive oil**
1 **onion**, chopped
1 small **baking potato**, about 5 oz, cut into small dice
1 **cauliflower**, trimmed and cut into pieces, about 1 lb prepared weight
2½ cups **vegetable stock**
1 teaspoon **English mustard**
3 teaspoons **Worcestershire sauce**
½ cup grated **Parmesan** or **sharp Cheddar cheese**
¾ cup **milk**
grated **nutmeg**
salt and **pepper**

To serve
⅔ cup **heavy cream**
croutons

Preheat the slow cooker if necessary; see the manufacturer's instructions. Heat the butter and oil in a large skillet, add the onion and potato, and fry for 5 minutes or until softened but not browned.

Stir in the cauliflower, stock, mustard, Worcestershire sauce, cheese, and a little salt and pepper and bring to a boil. Pour into the slow cooker pot, cover with the lid, and cook on low for 4–5 hours or until the vegetables are tender.

Puree the soup while still in the slow cooker pot with an immersion blender. Alternatively, transfer to a blender and puree, in batches if necessary, until smooth, then return to the slow cooker pot.

Stir in the milk, replace the lid, and cook on high for 15 minutes until reheated. Stir and add nutmeg to taste. Ladle the soup into bowls, swirl cream over the top, and sprinkle with a little extra grated nutmeg and some croutons.

For cheesy pumpkin soup, omit the cauliflower and add 1 lb peeled and seeded pumpkin or butternut squash. Dice the flesh and add to the fried onion and potato mixture. Continue as above.

light bites
& everyday
suppers

garlicky pork & sage pâté

Preparation time **30 minutes**,
   plus overnight chilling
Cooking temperature **high**
Cooking time **5–6 hours**
Serves **6–8**

1 tablespoon **olive oil**, plus
   extra for greasing
1 bunch of **sage**
1 small **onion**, chopped
13 oz or 6 **Toulouse
   sausages**, skins slit and
   removed
3 oz **bacon**, diced
7 oz boneless **belly pork
   slices**, finely diced
5 oz **chicken livers**, rinsed
   with cold water and drained
1 **egg**, beaten
2 tablespoons **sherry vinegar**
salt and **pepper**

Preheat the slow cooker if necessary; see the manufacturer's instructions. Oil a 3¾ cup rectangular heatproof dish and line with nonstick parchment paper, checking first that it will fit in the slow cooker pot. Cover the base with sage leaves, reserving the remainder.

Heat the oil in a skillet, add the onion, and fry until softened. Transfer to a bowl and add the sausages, bacon, and diced pork. Chop the drained chicken livers, discarding the white cores. Add to the bowl with the egg, vinegar, and salt and pepper. Mix together, then spoon half the mixture into the dish and press down firmly.

Arrange more sage leaves over the pâté, then cover with the remaining mixture. Press down firmly and arrange any remaining sage leaves on the top. Cover loosely with foil and stand the dish in the slow cooker pot. Pour boiling water into the pot to come halfway up the sides of the dish. Cover with the lid or foil, and cook on high for 5–6 hours or until the meat juices run clear when the center of the pâté is pierced with a knife.

Lift the dish out of the slow cooker pot using a dish towel, pour off the excess fat, stand the dish on a plate, then cover the top with a second plate and weigh down with measuring weights. Allow to cool, then transfer to the refrigerator overnight.

To serve, remove the weights, plate, and foil. Loosen the edges of the pâté with a knife, then turn out on to a cutting board and peel off the lining paper. Cut into slices and serve with toasted bread and salad.

red pepper & chorizo tortilla

Preparation time **20 minutes**
Cooking temperature **high**
Cooking time **2–2½ hours**
Serves **4**

1 tablespoon **olive oil**, plus
   extra for greasing
1 small **onion**, chopped
3 oz **chorizo**, diced
6 **eggs**
⅔ cup **milk**
½ cup roasted **red bell
   pepper** (from a jar), drained
   and sliced
8 oz cooked **potatoes**, sliced
salt and **pepper**

Preheat the slow cooker if necessary; see the manufacturer's instructions. Lightly oil a 5 cup soufflé dish and base-line with a circle of nonstick parchment paper, checking first that the dish will fit in the slow cooker pot.

Heat the oil in a skillet, add the onion and chorizo, and fry for 4–5 minutes until the onion is softened. Beat the eggs, milk, and a little salt and pepper in a bowl, then add the onion and chorizo, the red pepper, and sliced potatoes and mix together.

Tip the mixture into the oiled dish, cover the top with foil, and stand the dish in the slow cooker pot. Pour boiling water into the pot to come halfway up the sides of the dish. Cover with the lid and cook on high for 2–2½ hours or until the egg mixture has set in the center.

Lift the dish out of the slow cooker pot using a dish towel and remove the foil. Loosen the edge of the tortilla with a knife, turn it out onto a plate, and peel off the lining paper. Cut into slices and serve hot or cold with salad.

For cheesy bacon & rosemary tortilla, replace the chorizo with 3 oz diced bacon and fry with the onion as above. Beat the eggs and milk in a bowl with the chopped leaves from 2 small rosemary sprigs and 4 tablespoons freshly grated Parmesan or Cheddar cheese and salt and pepper. Replace the red pepper with 1 cup sliced button mushrooms and continue as above.

baked eggs on toast

Preparation time **15 minutes**
Cooking temperature **high**
Cooking time **40–50 minutes**
Serves **4**

2 tablespoons **butter**
4 wafer thin slices of **honey roast ham**, about 2½ oz in total
4 teaspoons **spicy tomato chutney**
4 **eggs**
2 **cherry tomatoes**, halved
1 **scallion**, finely sliced
salt and **pepper**
4 slices of **buttered toast**, to serve

Preheat the slow cooker if necessary; see the manufacturer's instructions. Grease 4 heatproof dishes, each ⅔ cup, with a little of the butter, checking first they will fit in the slow cooker pot, then press a slice of ham into each to line the base and sides, leaving a small overhang of ham above the dish.

Add 1 teaspoon of chutney to the base of each dish, then break an egg on top. Add a cherry tomato half to each, sprinkle with the scallion and a little salt and pepper, then dot with the remaining butter.

Cover each one with a square of foil and put the dishes into the slow cooker pot. Pour boiling water into the pot to come halfway up the sides of the dishes. Cover with the lid and cook on high for 40–50 minutes or until the egg whites are set and the yolks still slightly soft.

Lift the dishes out of the slow cooker pot using a dish towel and remove the foil. Loosen between the ham and the edge of the dishes with a knife and turn out. Quickly turn the baked eggs the right way up and arrange each one on a plate with hot buttered toast fingers.

For eggs Benedict, butter 4 dishes as above, then break an egg into each one, sprinkle with salt and pepper, the sliced scallion, and remaining butter. Cover with foil and cook as above. To serve, broil 8 Canadian bacon slices until golden. Toast 4 halved English breakfast muffins, spread with butter, divide the bacon between the lower halves, and arrange on serving plates. Top with the baked eggs and remaining muffin halves and serve drizzled with ⅔ cup warmed ready-made hollandaise sauce.

fish terrine

Preparation time **30 minutes**,
  plus cooling
Cooking temperature **high**
Cooking time **3–4 hours**
Serves **6–8**

oil, for greasing
12 oz boneless **haddock** or
  cod loin, cubed
2 **egg whites**
grated zest of ½ **lemon**
juice of 1 **lemon**
1 cup **heavy cream**
4 oz sliced **smoked salmon**
  or **trout**
5 oz **salmon** or **trout fillet**,
  thinly sliced
salt and **pepper**

Preheat the slow cooker if necessary; see the manufacturer's instructions. Lightly oil a 4 cup soufflé dish and base-line with a circle of nonstick parchment paper, checking first that the dish will fit in the slow cooker pot. Blend the haddock or cod loin, egg whites, lemon zest, half the lemon juice, and salt and pepper in a food processor until roughly chopped, then gradually add the cream and blend until just beginning to thicken.

Arrange half the smoked fish slices over the base of the dish. Spoon in half the fish mousse and spread it level. Mix the fish fillet with a little remaining lemon juice and some pepper, then arrange on top. Top with the remaining fish mousse, then the smoked fish slices.

Cover the top with foil and lower into the slow cooker pot. Pour boiling water into the pot to come halfway up the sides of the dish. Cover with the lid and cook on high for 3–4 hours or until the fish is cooked through and the terrine is set.

Lift the dish out of the slow cooker pot using a dish towel and allow to cool for 2 hours. Loosen the edge, turn out onto a plate and peel off the lining paper. Cut into thick slices and serve with salad and toast.

For smoked haddock & chive terrine make up the white fish mousse as above and flavor with 4 tablespoons chopped chives, 2 tablespoons chopped capers, and the grated zest and juice of half a lemon. Omit the smoked fish and arrange 1 sliced tomato over the base of the dish. Cover with half the fish mousse, 5 oz thinly sliced smoked cod fillet, then the remaining fish mousse. Continue as above.

warm lentil & feta salad

Preparation time **20 minutes**
Cooking temperature **high**
Cooking time **3–4 hours**
Serves **4**

¾ cup **puy lentils**
1 **onion**, chopped
1 **red bell pepper**, cored,
    seeded, and sliced
1 cup **cherry tomatoes**
2½ cups boiling **water**
2 tablespoons **tomato paste**
2 sprigs of **thyme**
4 tablespoons **olive oil**
2 tablespoons **balsamic
    vinegar**
2½ cups **watercress, spinach,
    and arugula salad**
5 oz **feta cheese**, crumbled
small bunch of **mint**, leaves
    stripped from the stems
salt and **pepper**

Preheat the slow cooker if necessary; see the manufacturer's instructions. Put the lentils into a strainer, rinse well with cold water, drain, and add to the slow cooker pot along with the onion, red pepper, and tomatoes.

Mix the boiling stock with the tomato paste, thyme, and a generous amount of salt and pepper. Pour over the lentils, cover with the lid, and cook on high for 3–4 hours or until the lentils are tender.

When almost ready to serve, fork the oil and balsamic vinegar together in a bowl, add the salad leaves, and toss gently. Spoon the hot lentils into shallow bowls, draining off any excess cooking liquid. Pile the salad on top and sprinkle with the feta, mint leaves, and a little extra pepper. Serve immediately with warm pita breads. Alternatively, lift the pot out of the housing using oven mitts, leave the lentils to go cold, then make the dressing and toss together with the leaves, feta, and mint.

For lentil salad with sardines & peas, cook the lentils as above, adding ⅔ cup frozen peas for the last 15 minutes of cooking time. Drain 2 x 3¾ oz cans sardines in tomato sauce, reserving the sauce. Flake the fish into chunky pieces, discarding the bones. Stir the sauce into the lentils. Shred 2 small crisphead lettuces and mix with ½ finely chopped red onion, then toss with the juice of 1 lemon, a small bunch of roughly chopped mint, and salt and pepper. Spoon the hot lentils into shallow bowls, top with the sardines and the lettuce salad. Serve immediately.

duck, pork, & apple rillettes

Preparation time **30 minutes**, plus cooling and overnight chilling
Cooking temperature **high**
Cooking time **5–6 hours**
Serves **4**

2 **duck legs**
1 lb rindless **belly pork slices**, halved
1 **onion**, cut into wedges
1 sharp **dessert apple**, such as Granny Smith, peeled, cored, and thickly sliced
2–3 sprigs of **thyme**
1 cup **chicken stock**
⅔ cup **hard cider**
salt and **pepper**

Preheat the slow cooker if necessary; see the manufacturer's instructions. Put the duck and belly pork into the base of the slow cooker pot. Tuck the onion and apple between the pieces of meat and add the thyme.

Pour the stock and cider into a saucepan and add plenty of salt and pepper. Bring to a boil, then pour into the slow cooker pot. Cover with the lid and cook on high for 5–6 hours or until the duck and pork are cooked through and tender.

Lift the meat out of the slow cooker pot with a slotted spoon and transfer to a large plate, then let cool for 30 minutes. Peel away the duck skin and remove the bones. Shred the meat into small pieces and discard the thyme sprigs. Scoop out the apple and onion with a slotted spoon, finely chop and mix with the meat, then taste and add more salt and pepper, if needed.

Pack the chopped meat mix into 4 individual dishes or small "le parfait" jars and press down firmly. Spoon over the juices from the slow cooker pot to cover and seal the meat. Allow to cool, then transfer to the refrigerator and chill well.

When the fat has solidified on the top, cover each dish with a lid or plastic wrap and store in the refrigerator for up to 1 week. Serve the rillettes with warm crusty bread, a few radishes, and pickled shallots, if desired.

For chicken, pork, & prune rillettes, omit the duck and put 2 chicken leg joints into the slow cooker pot with the pork belly slices, onion, and thyme, replacing the apple with ½ cup ready-to-eat pitted prunes. Continue as above.

turkey & cranberry meatloaf

Preparation time **30 minutes**, plus overnight chilling

Cooking temperature **high**

Cooking time **5–6 hours**

Serves **4–6**

1 tablespoon **sunflower oil**, plus extra for greasing

7 oz **bacon slices**

1 cup pack dried **orange and cranberry stuffing mix**

3 tablespoons dried **cranberries**

1 **onion**, finely chopped

1 lb skinless **turkey breast steaks**

1 **egg**, beaten

salt and **pepper**

Preheat the slow cooker if necessary; see the manufacturer's instructions. Lightly oil a soufflé dish, 5½ inches in diameter and 3½ inches high, and base-line with nonstick parchment paper, checking first that the dish will fit in the slow cooker pot. Stretch each bacon slice with the flat of a large cook's knife, until half as long again, and use about three-quarters of the slices to line the base and sides of the dish, trimming to fit.

Put the stuffing mix in a bowl, add the cranberries, and mix with boiling water according to the package instructions. Heat the oil in a skillet, add the onion, and fry for 5 minutes, stirring, until softened. Set aside. Finely chop the turkey slices in a food processor or pass through a coarse mincer.

Mix the stuffing with the fried onion, chopped turkey, and egg. Season well with salt and pepper and spoon into the bacon-lined dish. Press flat and cover with the remaining bacon slices. Cover the top of the dish with foil and lower into the slow cooker pot. Pour boiling water into the pot to come halfway up the sides of the dish. Cover with the lid and cook on high for 5–6 hours or until the juices run clear when the center of the meatloaf is pierced with a knife.

Lift the dish out of the slow cooker pot using a dish towel and allow to cool. Transfer to the refrigerator to chill overnight until firm. Loosen the edge of the meatloaf with a knife, turn out onto a plate, and peel off the lining paper. Cut into thick slices and serve with salad and spoonfuls of cranberry sauce or Beet Chutney (see pages 214–215), if desired.

zucchini & fava bean frittata

Preparation time **15 minutes**
Cooking temperature **high**
Cooking time **1½–2 hours**
Serves **4**

3 tablespoons **butter**
4 **scallions**, sliced
1 **zucchini**, about 7 oz, thinly sliced
⅔ cup podded fresh **fava beans**
6 **eggs**
1 cup **sour cream**
2 teaspoons chopped **tarragon**
2 tablespoons chopped **parsley**
salt and **pepper**

Preheat the slow cooker if necessary; see the manufacturer's instructions. Heat the butter, scallions and zucchini in a saucepan or in a bowl in the microwave until the butter has melted.

Line the slow cooker pot with nonstick parchment paper, tip in the zucchini and butter mix, then add the fava beans. Fork together the eggs, sour cream, herbs, and a little salt and pepper in a bowl, then pour into the pot. Cover with the lid and cook on high for 1½–2 hours or until set in the middle.

Lift the pot out of the housing using oven mitts. Loosen the edge of the frittata with a knife, carefully turn out onto a large plate, and peel off the lining paper. Cut the frittata into wedges and serve with salad and spoonfuls of Beet Chutney (see pages 214–215), if desired.

For zucchini, salmon, & asparagus frittata, add 1 cup sliced asparagus tips to the butter, scallions, and zucchini when heating and replace the fava beans with 4 oz chopped smoked salmon. Continue as above.

chilied corn

Preparation time **15 minutes**
Cooking temperature **high**
Cooking time **2–3 hours**
Serves **4**

1 tablespoon **sunflower oil**
1 **onion**, finely chopped
1 **orange bell pepper**, cored,
    seeded, and diced
⅔ cup frozen **corn kernels**,
    thawed
1 **garlic clove**, finely chopped
large pinch of **dried red
    pepper flakes**
½ teaspoon **ground cumin**
1 teaspoon **ground coriander**
13½ oz can **mixed beans**
13 oz can **chopped tomatoes**
⅔ cup **vegetable stock**
2 teaspoons **brown sugar**
salt and **pepper**

To serve
8 tablespoons **sour cream**
grated **cheddar cheese**

Preheat the slow cooker if necessary; see the manufacturer's instructions. Heat the oil in a large skillet, add the onion, and fry for 5 minutes, stirring, until softened.

Stir in the pepper, corn, garlic, and spices and cook for 1 minute. Add the beans, tomatoes, stock, sugar, and a little salt and pepper and bring to a boil.

Pour the mixture into the slow cooker pot, cover with the lid, and cook on high for 2–3 hours or until cooked through. Spoon into bowls and serve with sour cream and cheese, or spoon on top of baked potatoes.

For chilied mushrooms, fry the onion as above then add 8 oz quartered closed cup mushrooms instead of the bell pepper and corn, fry for 2–3 minutes, then add the garlic and spices and continue as above.

roasted vegetable terrine

Preparation time **30 minutes**,
plus cooling
Cooking temperature **high**
Cooking time **2–3 hours**
Serves **4**

12 oz **zucchini**, thinly sliced
1 **red bell pepper**, cored,
seeded, and quartered
1 **orange bell pepper**, cored,
seeded, and quartered
2 tablespoons **olive oil**, plus
extra for greasing
1 **garlic clove**, finely chopped
2 **eggs**
⅔ cup **milk**
¼ cup grated **Parmesan
cheese**
3 tablespoons chopped **basil**
salt and **pepper**

Preheat the slow cooker if necessary; see the
manufacturer's instructions. Line the broiler rack with foil.
Arrange all the vegetables on the foil in a single layer,
with the peppers skin side up. Drizzle with the oil and
sprinkle with the garlic and salt and pepper. Broil for
10 minutes or until softened and browned. Transfer the
zucchini slices to a plate and wrap the peppers in the foil.
Allow to stand for 5 minutes to loosen the skins.

Oil a 1 lb loaf pan and line the base and two long
sides with nonstick parchment paper, checking first it
will fit in the slow cooker pot. Beat together the eggs,
milk, Parmesan, basil, and salt and pepper in a bowl.
Unwrap the peppers, peel away the skins with a knife.

Arrange one-third of the zucchini slices over the base
of the tin. Spoon in a little of the custard, then add the
peppers and a little more custard. Repeat, ending with
a layer of zucchini and custard. Cover the top with foil
and put in the slow cooker pot. Pour boiling water into
the pot to come halfway up the sides of the pan. Cover
with the lid and cook on high for 2–3 hours or until the
custard is set.

Lift out the pan using a dish towel and allow to cool.
Loosen the edges with a knife, turn out onto a cutting
board and peel off the lining paper. Cut into slices and
serve with romesco sauce (see below).

For romesco sauce to accompany the terrine, fry
1 chopped onion in 1 tablespoon olive oil until softened.
Mix in 2 chopped garlic cloves, 4 skinned and chopped
tomatoes, ½ teaspoon paprika, and ½ cup finely
chopped almonds. Simmer for 10 minutes until thick.

irish stew

Preparation time **20 minutes**
Cooking temperature **high**
Cooking time **6–7 hours**
Serves **4**

2 tablespoons **sunflower oil**
2 lb **stewing lamb** or **budget lamb chops** of different sizes
1 **onion**, roughly chopped
3 **carrots**, sliced
1¾ cups diced **rutabaga**
1¾ cups diced **parsnips**
2 tablespoons **all-purpose flour**
13 oz **potatoes**, cut into chunks no bigger than 1½ inch square
3¼ cups **lamb** or **chicken stock**
3 sprigs of **rosemary**
salt and **pepper**
4 tablespoons mixed chopped **chives** and **rosemary**, to garnish

Preheat the slow cooker if necessary; see the manufacturer's instructions. Heat the oil in a large skillet, add the lamb, and fry until browned on both sides. Scoop out of the pan with a slotted spoon and transfer to a plate.

Add the onion to the pan and fry for 5 minutes or until softened. Add the carrots, rutabaga, and parsnips and cook for 1–2 minutes, then stir in the flour. Add the potatoes, stock, rosemary, and plenty of salt and pepper and bring to a boil, stirring.

Pour into the slow cooker pot, add the lamb and press below the surface of the liquid. Cover with the lid and cook on high for 6–7 hours or until the lamb is falling off the bones and the potatoes are tender.

Spoon into shallow bowls, removing the lamb bones if desired, and sprinkle with the chopped chives and rosemary. Serve with a spoon and fork and some crusty bread.

For lamb stew with dumplings, make up the stew as above. About 35–50 minutes before the end of cooking, mix 1¼ cups self-rising flour, ½ cup vegetable suet, 2 teaspoons chopped rosemary leaves, and a little salt and pepper in a bowl. Stir in 5–7 tablespoons water to make a soft but not sticky dough. Shape into 12 balls, add to the slow cooker pot, cover, and cook on high for 30–45 minutes until well risen.

moroccan meatballs

Preparation time **30 minutes**
Cooking temperature **low**
Cooking time **6–8 hours**
Serves **4**

1 lb **ground turkey**
½ cup drained canned **green
  lentils**
1 **egg yolk**
1 tablespoon **olive oil**
1 **onion**, sliced
2 **garlic cloves**, finely
  chopped
1 teaspoon **turmeric**
1 teaspoon **ground coriander**
½ teaspoon **ground cumin**
½ teaspoon **ground cinnamon**
1 inch **fresh ginger root**,
  peeled and finely chopped
13 oz can **chopped tomatoes**
⅔ cup **chicken stock**
salt and **pepper**

Preheat the slow cooker if necessary; see the manufacturer's instructions. Mix together the ground turkey, green lentils, a little salt and pepper, and the egg yolk in a bowl or food processor. Divide into 20 pieces, then shape into small balls with wetted hands.

Heat the oil in a large skillet, add the meatballs, and fry, stirring, until browned but not cooked through. Lift out of the pan with a slotted spoon and put into the slow cooker pot. Add the onion and fry until softened, then stir in the garlic, spices, and ginger and cook for 1 minute.

Stir in the tomatoes, stock, and a little salt and pepper and bring to a boil, stirring. Pour over the meatballs, cover with the lid, and cook on low for 6–8 hours or until cooked through. Stir, then spoon onto couscous-lined plates (see below).

For lemon couscous to accompany the meatballs, put 1 cup couscous into a bowl, pour over 1¾ cups boiling water, the grated zest and juice of 1 lemon, 2 tablespoons olive oil, and some salt and pepper. Cover and allow to stand for 5 minutes. Fluff up with a fork and stir in a small bunch of chopped cilantro.

chicken & sage hotpot

Preparation time **30 minutes**
Cooking temperature **high**
Cooking time **4–5 hours**
Serves **4**

1 tablespoon **sunflower oil**
6 boneless, skinless **chicken thighs**, about 1 lb, each cut into 3 pieces
1 **onion**, sliced
4 **bacon slices**, diced
2 tablespoons **all-purpose flour**
2½ cups **chicken stock** or a mix of **stock** and **hard cider**
2–3 sprigs of **sage**
4 oz **blood sausage**, diced (optional)
1⅓ cups diced **carrots**
1⅓ cups diced **rutabaga**
1¼ lb **potatoes**, thinly sliced
2 tablespoons **butter**
salt and **pepper**

Preheat the slow cooker if necessary; see the manufacturer's instructions. Heat the oil in a large skillet, add the chicken a few pieces at a time until all the meat is in the pan, then add the onion and bacon and fry, stirring, until the chicken is golden.

Stir in the flour, then gradually mix in the stock. Add the sage sprigs and a little salt and pepper and bring to a boil, stirring. Add the blood sausage, if using, carrots, and rutabaga to the slow cooker pot.

Pour over the hot chicken mixture, then arrange the potatoes overlapping on the top and press below the surface of the liquid. Sprinkle with a little extra salt and pepper, then cover with the lid and cook on high for 4–5 hours or until the potatoes are tender and the chicken is cooked through.

Lift the pot out of the housing using oven mitts, dot the potatoes with butter, and brown under a hot broiler. Spoon into shallow dishes to serve.

For mustardy beef hotpot, replace the chicken with 1½ lb trimmed and diced stewing beef. Fry the beef in the oil and transfer to the slow cooker pot, then fry the onion, omitting the bacon. Stir in the flour, then mix in 2½ cups beef stock, 2 teaspoons English mustard, 1 tablespoon Worcestershire sauce, 1 tablespoon tomato paste, and salt and pepper and bring to a boil. Omit the blood sausage and continue as above.

baked mackerel with beets

Preparation time **20 minutes**
Cooking temperature **high**
Cooking time **1½–2 hours**
Serves **4**

2 tablespoons **olive oil**
1 **onion**, sliced
1 **celery stick**, sliced
1 **carrot**, thinly sliced
2 tablespoons **light brown sugar**
4 tablespoons **cider vinegar**
¾ cup **fish stock**
2 **bay leaves**
4 **cloves**
1¼ cups cooked sliced **beets**
1 **dessert apple**, peeled, cored, and sliced
4 **mackerel**, each about 7 oz, gutted, heads removed, and rinsed in cold water

Mustard cream
2 teaspoons **whole grain mustard**
6 tablespoons **sour cream**
2 tablespoons chopped **chives**, plus extra to garnish
salt and **pepper**

Preheat the slow cooker if necessary; see the manufacturer's instructions. Heat the oil in a skillet, add the onion, celery, and carrot and fry for about 5 minutes or until softened.

Add the sugar, vinegar, fish stock, bay leaves, cloves, and a little salt and pepper and bring to a boil. Arrange the beets in the base of the slow cooker pot, then top with the apples. Slash the fish two or three times on each side, then arrange in a single layer on top of the apples.

Pour over the hot stock and vegetables, cover with the lid, and cook on high for 1½–2 hours or until the fish flakes easily when pressed in the center with a knife.

When almost ready to serve, mix together the ingredients for the mustard cream in a small bowl. Carefully transfer the fish, vegetables, and some of the stock to shallow bowls, then garnish with chives. Serve with spoonfuls of the mustard cream and crusty sliced bread.

For baked mackerel with hot potato salad, make up the recipe as above, omitting the beets. When the fish is almost ready, cook 13 oz baby new potatoes in a saucepan of boiling water for 15 minutes or until just tender. Make the mustard cream as above and toss with the hot potatoes. Serve with drained mackerel and sliced pickled cucumbers.

turkey & sausage stew

Preparation time **30 minutes**
Cooking temperature **high**
Cooking time **5½–6¾ hours**
Serves **4**

1 **turkey drumstick**, about
  1 lb 6 oz
2 tablespoons **sunflower oil**
4 **bacon slices**, diced
3 large **pork and herb
  sausages**, about 7 oz in total,
  each cut into 4 pieces
1 **onion**, sliced
1 **leek**, sliced; white and
  green parts kept separate
2 tablespoons **all-purpose
  flour**
2½ cups **chicken stock**
small bunch of **mixed herbs**
10 oz **baby carrots**, halved if
  large
2 **celery sticks**, sliced
½ cup fresh **cranberries**
salt and **pepper**

Parsley dumplings
1¼ cups **self-rising flour**
½ cup **shredded suet**
4 tablespoons chopped
  parsley
5–7 tablespoons **water**

Preheat the slow cooker if necessary; see the manufacturer's instructions. If the turkey drumstick does not fit into the slow cooker pot sever the knuckle end with a large heavy knife, hitting it with a rolling pin.

Heat the oil in a large skillet, add the drumstick, bacon, and sausage pieces and fry, turning until browned all over. Transfer to the slow cooker pot. Add the onion and white leeks slices to the pan and fry until softened. Stir in the flour, then mix in the stock. Add the herbs, salt and pepper, and bring to a boil.

Add the carrots, celery, and cranberries to the pot and pour over the hot onion mixture. Cover with the lid and cook on high for 5–6 hours or until the turkey is almost falling off the bone. Lift the turkey out of the slow cooker pot. Remove and discard the skin, then cut the meat into pieces, discarding the bones and tendons. Return meat to the pot with the reserved green leek slices.

Make the dumplings. Mix the flour, suet, parsley, and salt and pepper in a bowl. Stir in enough water to make a soft dough. Knead, then shape into 12 small balls. Arrange over the turkey, replace the lid and cook, still on high, for 30–45 minutes or until the dumplings are cooked through. Spoon into shallow bowls to serve.

For turkey & cranberry puff pie, make the stew as above. Roll out 1 lb puff pastry, trim to an oval a little larger than the top of the slow cooker pot, and put on an oiled baking sheet. Brush the top with beaten egg, then bake in a preheated oven at 400°F for about 25 minutes until golden. Spoon the stew onto plates and top with wedges of the pastry.

indian spiced cottage pie

Preparation time **30 minutes**
Cooking temperature **low**
Cooking time **8–10 hours**
Serves **4**

1 tablespoon **sunflower oil**
1 lb lean **ground beef**
1 **onion**, chopped
4 tablespoons **korma curry paste**
1 teaspoon **turmeric**
2 **carrots**, diced
2 tablespoons **all-purpose flour**
½ cup **red lentils**
⅓ cup **golden raisins**
1 tablespoon **tomato paste**
3¾ cups **beef stock**
salt and **pepper**

Topping
1¾ lb **potatoes**, cut into chunks
¼ cup **butter**
3 tablespoons **milk**
1 tablespoon **sunflower oil**
1 bunch of **scallions**, chopped
½ teaspoon **turmeric**

Preheat the slow cooker if necessary; see the manufacturer's instructions. Heat the oil in a large skillet, add the beef and onion, breaking up and stirring the meat until it is evenly browned. Stir in the curry paste and turmeric and cook for 1 minute. Stir in the carrots and flour, then add the lentils, golden raisins, tomato paste, stock, and salt and pepper. Bring to a boil, stirring, then pour into the slow cooker pot. Cover with the lid and cook on low for 8–10 hours or until the lentils are soft and the beef is tender.

When almost ready to serve, put the potatoes in a saucepan of boiling water and simmer for 15 minutes or until tender. Drain and mash with half the butter, milk, and salt and pepper. Heat the oil in a skillet, add the scallions, and fry for 2–3 minutes or until softened. Add the turmeric and cook for 1 minute, then mix into the mash.

Stir the beef mixture and lift the pot out of the housing using oven mitts. Transfer to a serving dish if desired. Spoon the mash on top, dot with remaining butter, then broil until golden. Serve with cooked peas.

For traditional cottage pie, fry the beef and onion as above. Omit the curry paste and turmeric. Add the carrots and flour, then replace the lentils and golden raisins with a 13 oz can baked beans, 1 tablespoon tomato paste, 1 tablespoon Worcestershire sauce, 1¼ cups beef stock, and 1 teaspoon dried mixed herbs. Transfer to the slow cooker pot and continue as above. Top with the mash, omitting the scallions and turmeric. Spoon over the meat, sprinkle with ½ cup grated cheddar cheese, and broil.

sausage tagliatelle

Preparation time **25 minutes**
Cooking temperature **low**
Cooking time **8–10 hours**
Serves **4**

1 tablespoon **sunflower oil**
8 **chili** or **spicy sausages**
1 **onion**, chopped
2 cups sliced **cup
mushrooms**
2 **garlic cloves**, finely
chopped
13 oz can **chopped tomatoes**
⅔ cup **beef stock**
8 oz **tagliatelle**
salt and **pepper**

To serve
basil leaves
freshly grated **Parmesan
cheese** (optional)

Preheat the slow cooker if necessary; see the
manufacturer's instructions. Heat the oil in a large
skillet, add the sausages and fry, turning until browned
but not cooked through. Transfer to the slow cooker pot
with tongs.

Drain off the excess fat from the pan to leave
2 teaspoons, then add the onion and fry until softened.
Mix in the mushrooms and garlic and fry for another
1–2 minutes.

Stir in the chopped tomatoes, stock, and a little salt
and pepper and bring to a boil, stirring. Pour the mixture
over the sausages, cover with the lid, and cook on low
for 8–10 hours or until cooked through.

When almost ready to serve, bring a large saucepan
of water to a boil, add the tagliatelle, and cook for
7–8 minutes or until just tender then drain. Lift the
sausages out of the slow cooker pot and slice thickly,
then return to the pot with the pasta and mix together.
Sprinkle with torn basil leaves and grated Parmesan,
if desired. Serve with a green salad.

For chicken & chorizo tagliatelle, omit the
sausages and fry 1 lb diced boneless chicken thighs
in 1 tablespoon olive oil until golden. Drain and
transfer to the slow cooker pot. Continue as above,
adding 4 oz diced chorizo sausage to the skillet with
the onions and replacing the beef stock with ⅔ cup
chicken stock.

chicken & navy bean stew

Preparation time **20 minutes**
Cooking temperature **low**
Cooking time **8–9 hours**
Serves **4**

2 tablespoons **olive oil**
1¼ lb boneless, skinless **chicken thighs**, cubed
1 **onion**, sliced
2 **garlic cloves**, finely chopped
2 tablespoons **all-purpose flour**
2½ cups **chicken stock**
1 **red bell pepper**, cored, seeded, and sliced
7 oz can **corn kernels**, drained
13½ oz can **navy beans**, drained
10 oz small **new potatoes**, scrubbed and thinly sliced
2 sprigs of **thyme**, plus extra to garnish (optional)
salt and **pepper**

Preheat the slow cooker if necessary; see the manufacturer's instructions. Heat the oil in a large skillet, add the chicken and onion and fry, stirring, until lightly browned.

Stir in the garlic and flour, then gradually mix in the stock. Add the red pepper, corn, navy beans, and new potatoes. Add the thyme and a little salt and pepper and bring to a boil, stirring.

Transfer the mixture to the slow cooker pot and press the chicken and potatoes below the surface of the liquid. Cover with the lid and cook on low for 8–9 hours or until the chicken is cooked through and the potatoes are tender.

Stir well, then spoon into shallow bowls and sprinkle with a few extra thyme leaves, if desired. Serve with hot garlic bread.

For Spanish chicken with chorizo, fry the chicken and onion with 3 oz ready-diced chorizo until well browned, then mix in 1 teaspoon smoked paprika, the garlic, and flour. Continue as above, replacing the thyme with 2 rosemary sprigs. Serve sprinkled with chopped parsley.

ham & leek suet pudding

Preparation time **30 minutes**
Cooking temperature **high**
Cooking time **4–5 hours**
Serves **4**

2 tablespoons **butter**
2 **ham steaks**, about 1 lb in
   total, diced and any fat and
   rind discarded
8 oz **leeks**, trimmed, cleaned,
   and sliced
2½ cups **self-rising flour**
1¼ cups **vegetable suet**
3 teaspoons **powdered
   mustard**
¾–1 cup **water**
salt and **pepper**

Parsley sauce
2 tablespoons **butter**
¼ cup **all-purpose flour**
1¼ cups **milk**
⅛ cup **parsley**, finely chopped

Preheat the slow cooker if necessary; see the manufacturer's instructions. Heat the butter in a skillet, add the ham and leeks and fry, stirring, for 4–5 minutes or until the leeks have just softened. Season with pepper only. Allow to cool slightly.

Put the flour, ½ teaspoon salt, a large pinch of pepper, the suet, and powdered mustard in a bowl and mix well. Gradually stir in enough water to make a soft but not sticky dough. Knead lightly, then roll out on a large piece of floured nonstick parchment paper to a rectangle 9 x 12 inches. Turn the paper so that the shorter edges are facing you.

Spoon the ham mixture over the pastry, leaving ¾ inch around the edges. Roll up, starting at the shorter edge, using the paper to help. Wrap in the paper, then in a sheet of foil. Twist the ends together tightly, leaving some space for the pudding to rise.

Transfer the pudding to the slow cooker pot and raise off the base slightly by standing it on 2 ramekin dishes. Pour boiling water into the pot to come a little up the sides of the pudding, being careful that the water cannot seep through any joins. Cover with the lid and cook on high for 4–5 hours or until the pudding is well risen.

Just before serving, melt the butter for the sauce in a saucepan. Stir in the flour, then gradually mix in the milk and bring to a boil, stirring until smooth. Cook for 1–2 minutes, then stir in the parsley and season. Lift the pudding out of the slow cooker pot, unwrap, and cut into slices. Arrange on plates and spoon over a little sauce. Serve with sugar snap peas.

short-cut suppers

chicken & sweet potato balti

Preparation time **15 minutes**

Cooking temperature **high** and **low**

Cooking time **6–7 hours**

Serves **4**

6 boneless, skinless **chicken thighs**, about 1 lb in total, cubed

1 **onion**, sliced

12 oz **sweet potatoes**, cut into ¾ inch cubes

2 **garlic cloves**, finely chopped

1¾ cups **balti curry sauce**

chopped **cilantro**, to garnish (optional)

Preheat the slow cooker if necessary; see the manufacturer's instructions. Arrange the chicken, onion, and sweet potatoes in the base of the slow cooker pot in an even layer. Sprinkle with the garlic.

Bring the curry sauce just to a boil in a small saucepan or the microwave. Pour into the slow cooker pot in an even layer. Cover with the lid and cook on high for 30 minutes. Reduce the heat and cook on low for 5½–6½ hours, or set to auto for 6–7 hours, until the chicken is cooked through and the sauce piping hot.

Stir well, then sprinkle with roughly chopped cilantro, if desired. Spoon into bowls and serve with warmed naan bread.

For harissa baked chicken with sweet potato,

prepare the chicken and vegetables as above. Replace the balti curry sauce with 13 oz can chopped tomatoes and 2 teaspoons harissa paste. Continue as above.

balsamic braised pork chops

Preparation time **15 minutes**
Cooking temperature **high** and
  low
Cooking time **7–8 hours**
Serves **4**

4 **spare rib pork chops**,
  about 1½ lb in total
3 tablespoons **apple**
  balsamic or **plain balsamic**
  vinegar
2 tablespoons **light brown**
  sugar
2 **onions**, thinly sliced
2 **dessert apples**, peeled,
  cored, and quartered
2 tablespoons **cornstarch**
3 teaspoons **English mustard**
¾ cup boiling **chicken stock**
chopped **chives**, to garnish
  (optional)

Preheat the slow cooker if necessary; see the manufacturer's instructions. Put the pork chops into the base of the slow cooker pot and spoon over the vinegar and sugar. Sprinkle the onions on top, then add the apples.

Put the cornstarch and mustard in a small bowl and mix with a little cold water to make a smooth paste, then gradually stir in the boiling stock until smooth. Pour over the pork. Cover with the lid and cook on high for 30 minutes. Reduce the heat and cook on low for 6½–7½ hours, or set to auto for 7–8 hours, until the pork is cooked through and tender.

Transfer the pork to serving plates, stir the sauce, and spoon over the chops. Sprinkle with chopped chives, if desired, and serve with mashed potato and Brussel sprouts.

For cider-braised pork, prepare the pork chops as above, omitting the vinegar. Bring ¾ cup hard cider to a boil in a saucepan. Make up the cornstarch paste as above, then gradually stir in the boiling cider instead of the stock. Pour over the chops and continue as above.

baked seafood with saffron

Preparation time **15 minutes**
Cooking temperature **low** and **high**
Cooking time **5½–7½ hours**
Serves **4**

1 **onion**, finely chopped
1 **red bell pepper**, cored, seeded, and diced
2 **garlic cloves**, finely chopped
13 oz can **chopped tomatoes**
⅔ cup **dry white wine** or **fish stock**
large pinch of **saffron threads**
2 sprigs of **thyme**
1 tablespoon **olive oil**
13 oz frozen **seafood** (shrimp, mussels, squid), thawed
10 oz **tagliatelle**
salt and **pepper**
chopped **parsley**, to garnish

Preheat the slow cooker if necessary; see the manufacturer's instructions. Put the onion, red pepper, garlic, and tomatoes into the slow cooker pot, then add the wine or stock, saffron, thyme, oil, and a little salt and pepper.

Cover with the lid and cook on low for 5–7 hours. Rinse the seafood with cold water, drain, and then stir into the slow cooker pot. Replace the lid and cook on high for 30 minutes or until piping hot.

When almost ready to serve, bring a large saucepan of water to a boil, add the pasta, and cook for 8–10 minutes or until just tender. Drain and toss with the parsley. Spoon into shallow bowls and top with the seafood sauce.

For baked salmon with pesto, omit the seafood and drain a 13 oz can red salmon, remove the skin and bones, and break the fish into large flakes. Put the onion, red pepper, and garlic into the slow cooker pot. Heat the tomatoes and wine or stock in a small saucepan or the microwave, then add to the pot with 2 teaspoons pesto and the oil, omitting the saffron and thyme. Mix in the salmon and continue as above.

pot roast lamb with rosemary

Preparation time **5 minutes**
Cooking temperature **high**
Cooking time **7–8 hours**
Serves **4**

2–2 lb 7 oz **half lamb
shoulder on the bone**
3 sprigs of **rosemary**
1 **red onion**, cut into wedges
2 tablespoons **red currant
jelly**
1 cup **red wine**
1 cup **lamb stock**
salt and **pepper**

Preheat the slow cooker if necessary; see the manufacturer's instructions. Put the lamb into the slow cooker pot, add the rosemary on top and tuck the onion wedges around the sides of the joint.

Spoon the red currant jelly into a small saucepan and add the wine, stock, and a little salt and pepper. Bring to a boil, stirring so that the jelly melts, then pour over the lamb. Cover with the lid and cook on high for 7–8 hours or until a knife goes into the center of the lamb easily and the meat is almost falling off the bone.

Lift the joint out of the slow cooker pot and put it onto a serving plate with the onions. Discard the rosemary sprigs and pour the wine and stock mixture into a pitcher to serve as gravy. Carve the lamb onto plates and serve with steamed green vegetables and baby potatoes or crushed new potatoes with rosemary cream (see below).

For crushed new potatoes with rosemary cream

to accompany the lamb, bring a pan of water to a boil, add 1 lb baby new potatoes and cook for 15 minutes. Add 7 oz tenderstem broccoli, thickly sliced, for the last 5 minutes. Drain and then roughly break up with a fork. Stir in 1 tablespoon finely chopped rosemary, 4 tablespoons sour cream, and a little salt and pepper. Spoon a mound of potatoes into the center of 4 serving plates, then top with the carved pot roast lamb and drizzle the gravy around the edges of the potatoes.

honey-glazed ham

Preparation time **20 minutes**,
  plus overnight soaking
Cooking temperature **high**
Cooking time **5–7 hours**
Serves **4**

2 lb boneless **smoked ham**
  joint, soaked overnight in
  cold water
1 **onion**, cut into wedges
10 oz **carrots**, halved
  lengthwise and cut into
  1 inch chunks
1 lb medium **baking potatoes**,
  scrubbed and quartered
2 **bay leaves**
6 **cloves**
½ teaspoon **black
  peppercorns**
3¾ cups boiling **water**

Glaze
2 tablespoons **honey**
2 teaspoons **English mustard**

Preheat the slow cooker if necessary; see the manufacturer's instructions. Put the ham joint into the slow cooker pot. Tuck the vegetables around the sides, then add the bay leaves, cloves, and peppercorns. Pour over the boiling water to just cover the ham.

Cover with the lid and cook on high for 5–7 hours or until the ham and vegetables are cooked through and tender. Lift the ham out of the slow cooker pot and transfer to the base of a broiler pan. Cut away the rind and discard.

Mix the honey and mustard together for the glaze, spoon over the top and sides of the joint, then add 3 ladlefuls of stock from the slow cooker pot to the base of the broiler pan. Broil until the ham is golden brown. Carve into slices and serve with the sauce from the broiler pan and drained vegetables from the slow cooker pot. Accompany with steamed green beans, if desired.

For glazed ham with pease pudding, soak 1 cup dried yellow split peas in cold water overnight while soaking the ham in a separate bowl of cold water. Next day, drain the peas, add to a saucepan with 5 cups water, bring to a boil, and boil rapidly for 10 minutes. Add the ham joint, onion, carrots, bay leaves, cloves, and peppercorns to the slow cooker pot, omitting the potatoes. Pour in the hot peas and their water, then continue as above. When the glazed ham is broiled, drain off most of the stock from the peas and carrots, then mash and stir in 2 tablespoons butter and a little salt, if needed. Serve the pease pudding with the sliced ham.

keema mutter

Preparation time **10 minutes**
Cooking temperature **high** and **low**
Cooking time **8–10 hours**
Serves **4**

1 lb **lean ground beef**
1 **onion**, finely chopped
13 oz can **chopped tomatoes**
3 tablespoons **mild curry paste**
2 teaspoons **cumin seeds**
2–3 **bird's eye green chilies**, seeded and sliced
1 inch **fresh ginger root**, peeled and finely chopped
2 **garlic cloves**, finely chopped
2 oz **creamed coconut**, crumbled
½ cup boiling **beef stock**
1 cup frozen **peas**
chopped **cilantro** and extra sliced **chilies**, to garnish

Preheat the slow cooker if necessary; see the manufacturer's instructions. Put the beef, onion, and tomatoes into the slow cooker pot, then stir in the curry paste, cumin seeds, chili, ginger, and garlic. Sprinkle the coconut over the top, then stir in the boiling stock.

Cover with the lid and cook on high for 30 minutes. Reduce the heat and cook on low for 7–9 hours, or set to auto for 7½–9½ hours Stir the ground beef well to break up into small pieces, then mix in the peas and cook on high for 30 minutes or until cooked through.

When almost ready to serve, sprinkle with the chopped cilantro and sliced chilies. Serve with warmed chapattis and a tomato and red onion salad.

For keema aloo, make up the recipe as above, replacing the ground beef with 1 lb ground lamb. Stir in 7 oz potatoes, cut into small dice, after adding the garlic. At the end of cooking, replace the peas with 2½ cups washed, torn spinach. Serve sprinkled with 4 finely sliced scallions and a little chopped cilantro.

tomato-braised squid with chorizo

Preparation time **20 minutes**
Cooking temperature **low**
Cooking time **3½–5½ hours**
Serves **4**

1¼ lb chilled **squid**
1 **onion**, thinly sliced
4 oz ready-diced **chorizo**
4 oz **cup mushrooms**, sliced
1 **red bell pepper**, cored,
    seeded, and sliced
2 **garlic cloves**, finely
    chopped
2–3 sprigs of **rosemary**,
    leaves stripped from the
    stems
1 tablespoon **tomato paste**
1 teaspoon **superfine sugar**
13 oz can **chopped tomatoes**
6 tablespoons **red wine**
1 tablespoon **cornstarch**
salt and **pepper**
chopped **parsley**, to garnish

Preheat the slow cooker if necessary; see the manufacturer's instructions. Rinse the squid inside and out, pulling off the tentacles and reserving. Drain and slice the bodies. Put the tentacles in a bowl, cover with plastic wrap and chill in the refrigerator.

Put the onion, chorizo, mushrooms, and red pepper into the slow cooker pot. Add the garlic, rosemary, tomato paste and sugar, then stir in the sliced squid.

Pour the tomatoes and wine into a saucepan and bring to a boil or heat in the microwave. Add a little salt and pepper, then pour into the slow cooker pot and stir well. Cover with the lid and cook on low for 3–5 hours or until the squid is tender.

When almost ready to serve, put the cornstarch in a small bowl with a little cold water and mix to a smooth paste. Stir into the slow cooker pot, add the squid tentacles, then replace the lid and cook, still on low, for 30 minutes. Spoon into bowls and sprinkle with chopped parsley. Serve with thickly sliced bread or rice.

For tomato-braised squid with red onion, replace the onion, mushrooms, and chorizo with 2 large thinly sliced red onions and put in the slow cooker pot with the red pepper, garlic, tomato paste, and sugar, adding 2 bay leaves instead of the rosemary. Add the squid and continue as above.

hot spanish beans

Preparation time **10 minutes**
Cooking temperature **high**
Cooking time **4–5 hours**
Serves **4**

4 oz **chorizo**, sliced
1 **red onion**, chopped
2 x 13½ oz cans **navy beans**, drained
1½ cups **cherry tomatoes**
2 **garlic cloves**, finely chopped
2–3 sprigs of **rosemary**, leaves stripped from the stems
11½ oz package chilled **frankfurters**, drained and thickly sliced
½ cup marinated **mixed olives** (optional)
¾ cup boiling **vegetable stock**
1 tablespoon **tomato paste**
salt and **pepper**

Preheat the slow cooker if necessary; see the manufacturer's instructions. Put the chorizo, onion, and navy beans into the slow cooker pot, add the tomatoes, garlic, and rosemary and mix together. Arrange the frankfurters and olives, if using, on the top.

Mix the boiling stock with the tomato paste and a little salt and pepper, then pour into the slow cooker pot. Cover with the lid and cook on high for 4–5 hours. Stir the beans, then spoon into bowls. Serve with hot peppered foccacia or garlic bread and a green leafy salad.

For mustard beans, put the onion, beans, tomatoes, and garlic in the slow cooker pot, omitting the chorizo, rosemary, and olives. Add 1 cored, seeded, and diced red bell pepper. Mix the stock with 2 tablespoons tomato paste, 2 tablespoons Worcestershire sauce, 1 tablespoon Dijon mustard, ½ teaspoon smoked paprika, and salt and pepper. Pour over the beans and add the frankfurters. Continue as above.

pork with black bean sauce

Preparation time **20 minutes**,
plus overnight marinating
Cooking temperature **high** and
low
Cooking time **8–10 hours**
Serves **4**

4 **spare rib pork steaks**,
about 6 oz each
2 tablespoons **cornstarch**
4 tablespoons **soy sauce**
1½ inches **fresh ginger root**,
peeled and finely chopped
2 **garlic cloves**, finely
chopped
½ cup **black bean sauce**
1¼ cups boiling **chicken stock**
pepper

To serve
1 tablespoon **sunflower oil**
2 cups **mixed vegetable
stir-fry**
cooked **rice**

Put the pork steaks into a shallow nonmetallic dish.
Put the cornstarch and soy sauce in a small bowl and
mix to a smooth paste, then add the ginger, garlic,
black bean sauce, and a little pepper. Pour over the
pork, cover with plastic wrap and marinate in the
refrigerator overnight.

Preheat the slow cooker if necessary; see the
manufacturer's instructions. Put the pork and marinade
into the slow cooker pot. Pour over the boiling stock,
cover with the lid, and cook on high for 30 minutes.
Reduce the heat and cook on low for 7½–9½ hours,
or set to auto for 8–10 hours, until the pork is cooked
through and tender.

When almost ready to serve, heat the oil in a large
skillet, add the mixed vegetables and stir-fry for
2–3 minutes or until just tender. Spoon the pork onto
plates lined with rice and top with the vegetables.

For sweet & sour pork, omit the black bean sauce
from the marinade, add the marinated pork to the
slow cooker pot with 1 bunch of sliced scallions,
1 cored, seeded, and sliced red bell pepper, and
1 cup sliced mushrooms. Replace the chicken stock
with a 1¾ cups sweet and sour sauce. Bring the
sauce to a boil in a saucepan or the microwave, then
pour into the slow cooker pot. Continue as above.

fragrant spiced chicken with chili

Preparation time **15 minutes**
Cooking temperature **high**
Cooking time **5–6 hours**
Serves **4–5**

3 lb oven-ready whole
  chicken, rinsed with cold
  water, drained well
1 **onion**, chopped
1⅓ cups sliced **carrots**
3 inches **fresh ginger root**,
  peeled and sliced
2 **garlic cloves**, sliced
1 large **mild red chili**, halved
3 large **star anise**
4 tablespoons **soy sauce**
4 tablespoons **rice vinegar**
1 tablespoon **light brown
  sugar**
3¾ cups boiling **water**
small bunch of **cilantro**
7 oz dried **egg noodles**
¾ cup **snow peas**, thickly
  sliced
2 **bok choy**, about 5 oz,
  thickly sliced
salt and **pepper**

Preheat the slow cooker if necessary; see the manufacturer's instructions. Put chicken breast side down into the slow cooker pot. Add the onion, carrots, ginger, garlic, chili, and star anise and spoon over the soy sauce, vinegar, and sugar.

Pour over the boiling water. Cut the cilantro leaves from the stems; add the stems to the pot, reserving the leaves. Season with salt and pepper, cover with the lid, and cook on high for 5–6 hours or until the juices run clear when the thickest part of the leg is pierced with a knife.

When almost ready to serve, put the noodles into a large bowl, cover with boiling water, and allow to soak for 5 minutes. Lift the chicken out of the slow cooker pot, put onto a plate, cover with foil, and keep hot. Add the snow peas and bok choy to the pot, replace the lid, and cook, still on high, for 5–10 minutes or until just wilted.

Carve the chicken into bite-size pieces. Drain the noodles, divide between 4 bowls. Top with chicken and chopped cilantro leaves, then ladle over the hot broth.

For Italian spiced chicken with pesto, put the chicken into the pot with the onion, carrot, and garlic only and add 1 sliced fennel bulb and 1 sliced lemon. Continue as above, replacing the cilantro with basil. When the chicken is removed, add the snow peas, 3 chopped tomatoes, 5 oz chopped purple sprouting broccoli, and 2 tablespoons pesto sauce, cover, and cook for 5–10 minutes. Omit the bok choy. Put 8 oz fresh tagliatelle in a saucepan of boiling water and cook for 2 minutes. Drain and continue as above.

smoked cod with bean mash

Preparation time **15 minutes**
Cooking temperature **low**
Cooking time **1½–2 hours**
Serves **4**

2 x 13½ oz cans **cannellini
    beans**, drained
bunch of **scallions**, thinly
    sliced; white and green parts
    kept separate
1¾ cups boiling **fish stock**
1 teaspoon **whole grain
    mustard**
grated zest and juice of
    1 **lemon**
4 **smoked cod loins**, about
    1¼ lb in total
4 tablespoons **sour cream**
small bunch of **parsley**,
    watercress, or **arugula
    leaves**, roughly chopped
salt and **pepper**

Preheat the slow cooker if necessary; see the
manufacturer's instructions. Put the drained beans into
the slow cooker pot with the white scallion. Mix the fish
stock with the mustard, lemon zest and juice, and a
little salt and pepper, then pour into the pot.

Arrange the fish on top and sprinkle with a little
extra pepper. Cover with the lid and cook on low for
1½–2 hours or until the fish flakes easily when pressed
in the center with a knife.

Lift out the fish with a spatula and transfer to a plate.
Pour off nearly all the cooking liquid, then mash the
beans roughly. Stir in the sour cream, the remaining
scallion and the parsley, watercress, or arugula. Taste
and adjust the seasoning, if needed. Spoon the mash
on to plates and top with the fish.

For baked salmon with basil bean mash, add the
beans to the slow cooker pot with the ingredients as
above, omitting the mustard. Arrange 4 x 5 oz salmon
steaks on top, season, and cook as above. Mash the
beans with the sour cream, green scallions, and a
small bunch of roughly torn basil and serve with the
fish as above.

asian glazed ribs

Preparation time **25 minutes**,
plus overnight marinating
Cooking temperature **high** and
low
Cooking time **8–10 hours**,
plus 10–15 minutes grilling
Serves **4**

1 **onion**, quartered
2 inches **fresh ginger root**,
peeled and sliced
2 tablespoons **rice** or **white
wine vinegar**
4 **star anise**
1 **cinnamon stick**, halved
2½ lb **pork ribs**
4 cups boiling **water**
2 **breakfast tea bags**

Glaze
4 tablespoons **honey**
4 tablespoons **soy sauce**

Put the onion, ginger, vinegar, star anise, and cinnamon into a bowl and cover with plastic wrap. Chill in the refrigerator overnight.

Preheat the slow cooker if necessary; see the manufacturer's instructions. Pour the boiling water over the teabags and let brew for 2–3 minutes, then squeeze out the bags and discard. Rinse the ribs with cold water, drain, and put into the slow cooker pot with the spiced onion mix and the hot tea.

Cover with the lid and cook on high for 30 minutes. Reduce the heat and cook on low for 7½–9½ hours, or set to auto for 8–10 hours, until the meat is almost falling off the bones.

Lift the ribs out of the slow cooker pot and transfer to a foil-lined broiler pan. Put 6 tablespoons of stock from the pot into a bowl and mix in the honey and soy sauce. Spoon over the ribs, then broil for 10–15 minutes, turning several times and spooning soy mixture over until browned and glazed. Serve with pickled cucumber (see below) and rice.

For pickled cucumber to accompany the ribs, mix ¼–½ mild red chili, seeded and finely chopped, 3 tablespoons chopped cilantro, 1 tablespoon rice or white wine vinegar, 1 teaspoon fish sauce, and ½ teaspoon superfine sugar in a salad bowl. Very thinly slice ½ cucumber, add to the dressing, and toss together gently. This dish can be made, covered with plastic wrap and kept in the refrigerator overnight.

stifado

Preparation time **25 minutes**, plus overnight marinating
Cooking temperature **high and low**
Cooking time **10–11 hours**
Serves **4**

¾ cup **red wine**
1 tablespoon **tomato paste**
2 tablespoons **olive oil**
2–3 sprigs of **thyme** or bay leaves
4 **cloves**
¼ teaspoon **ground allspice**
10 oz **shallots**, halved if large
2 **garlic cloves**, finely chopped
1½ lb **stewing beef**, cut into large chunks and any fat discarded
4 teaspoons **cornstarch**
⅔ cup cold **water**
½ **bouillon cube**
salt and **pepper**

Mix the wine, tomato paste and oil in a shallow nonmetallic dish. Add the herbs, spices, and a little salt and pepper and mix together. Mix in the shallots and garlic, then add the beef and toss in the marinade. Cover with plastic wrap and marinate in the refrigerator overnight.

Preheat the slow cooker if necessary; see the manufacturer's instructions. Put the cornstarch into a saucepan, mix in a little of the water to make a smooth paste, then mix in the remaining water. Drain the marinade from the beef into the pan and crumble in the bouillon cube. Bring to a boil, stirring.

Tip the beef, shallots, and flavorings into the slow cooker pot and pour over the hot stock. Cover with the lid and cook on high for 30 minutes. Reduce the heat and cook on low for 9½–10½ hours, or set to auto for 10–11 hours, until the meat is cooked through and tender. Spoon into bowls and serve with toasted French bread and herb butter.

For lamb stifado, mix together ¾ cup white wine, 1 tablespoon tomato paste, 2 tablespoons olive oil, 2 bay leaves, 2 teaspoons roughly crushed cilantro seeds, and ½ sliced lemon, add the shallots and garlic, and stir in 1½ lb diced lamb shoulder or leg. Marinate overnight, then continue as above.

chicken avgolemono

Preparation time **30 minutes**
Cooking temperature **high and low**
Cooking time **6–8 hours**
Serves **4**

8 boneless, skinless **chicken thighs**, about 1 lb 6 oz in total, each cut into 3 or 4 pieces
1 **onion**, thinly sliced
2–3 sprigs of **oregano** or **basil**
1¾ cups boiling **chicken stock**
grated zest and juice of 1 **lemon**
10 oz **macaroni** or **orzo pasta**
2 **eggs**
2 **egg yolks**
4 tablespoons chopped **parsley**, plus extra to garnish (optional)
salt and **pepper**
lemon zest curls, to garnish (optional)

Preheat the slow cooker if necessary; see the manufacturer's instructions. Put the chicken, onion, and herbs into the slow cooker pot. Mix the stock, lemon zest and juice, and salt and pepper then pour over the chicken.

Cover with the lid and cook on high for 30 minutes. Reduce the heat and cook on low for 5½–7½ hours, or set to auto for 6–8 hours, until the chicken is cooked through and tender. When almost ready to serve, bring a large saucepan of water to a boil, add the pasta, and cook for 9–10 minutes or until just tender.

Meanwhile, drain the stock from the slow cooker pot into a second large saucepan and boil for 5 minutes until reduced by one-third or to about ¾ cup. Whisk the eggs and egg yolks in a bowl, then gradually whisk in 2 ladlefuls of stock until smooth. Pour into the reduced stock, then whisk over a gentle heat until the sauce has thickened slightly. Stir in the parsley.

Pour the sauce over the chicken. Spoon the pasta into shallow bowls and top with the chicken. Sprinkle with lemon rind curls and extra chopped parsley, if desired.

For salmon avgolemeno, lower a 1 lb thick piece of salmon into the slow cooker pot over a double thickness strip of foil, add 6 thinly sliced scallions and the oregano or basil. Pour over 1½ cups boiling fish stock mixed with the lemon zest and juice and salt and pepper. Cover and cook on low for 2½–3 hours or until the fish flakes easily when pressed in the center with a knife. Cook the pasta and make the sauce as above. Lift the salmon out with the foil, skin and flake into large chunks, then toss with the sauce and pasta.

vegetarian

mushroom & tomato rigatoni

Preparation time **20 minutes**
Cooking temperature **high**
Cooking time **2½–3 hours**
Serves **4**

8 oz **rigatoni** or **pasta quills**
3 tablespoons **olive oil**
1 **onion**, sliced
2–3 **garlic cloves**, finely chopped
8 oz **cup mushrooms**, sliced
8 oz **portabella mushrooms**, sliced
8 oz **tomatoes**, cut into chunks
13 oz can **chopped tomatoes**
¾ cup **vegetable stock** or **dry white wine**
1 tablespoon **tomato paste**
3 sprigs of **rosemary**
salt and **pepper**
freshly grated **Parmesan cheese**, to serve

Preheat the slow cooker if necessary; see the manufacturer's instructions. Put the pasta into a large bowl, cover with boiling water, and allow to stand for 10 minutes while preparing the rest of the dish.

Heat 1 tablespoon of the oil in a large skillet, add the onion and fry until softened. Stir in the remaining oil, garlic, and mushrooms and fry, stirring, until the mushrooms are just beginning to brown.

Stir in the fresh and canned tomatoes, stock or wine, and tomato paste. Add the rosemary and a little salt and pepper and bring to a boil.

Drain the pasta and put it in the slow cooker pot, pour over the hot mushroom mixture and spread into an even layer. Cover with the lid and cook on low for 2½–3 hours or until the pasta is just tender. Spoon into shallow bowls and sprinkle with grated Parmesan. Serve with an arugula salad.

For mushroom pastichio, replace the rigatoni or quills with 8 oz macaroni and continue as above. Mix 3 eggs with 1 cup plain yogurt, 3 oz grated feta cheese, and a pinch of grated nutmeg. Spoon over the top of the cooked mushroom and pasta mix for the last hour of cooking until set. Lift the pot out of the housing using oven mitts and brown under a hot broiler.

vegetable goulash

Preparation time **20 minutes**
Cooking temperature **high**
Cooking time **4–5 hours**
Serves **4**

1 tablespoon **sunflower oil**
1 **onion**, chopped
1½ cups diced **rutabaga**
1½ cups diced **carrots**
1½ cups diced **potatoes**
1 **red bell pepper**, cored,
   seeded, and diced
2 **celery sticks**, sliced
5 oz **cup mushrooms**, halved
1 teaspoon **smoked paprika**,
   plus extra to garnish
   (optional)
¼ teaspoon **dried red pepper
   flakes**
1 teaspoon **caraway seeds**
1 tablespoon **all-purpose
   flour**
13 oz can **chopped tomatoes**
1¼ cups **vegetable stock**
2 **bay leaves**
salt and **pepper**
⅔ cup **sour cream**, to serve

Preheat the slow cooker if necessary; see the manufacturer's instructions. Heat the oil in a large skillet, add the onion and fry, stirring, until softened. Add the vegetables, fry for 1–2 minutes, then stir in the paprika, pepper flakes, and caraway seeds and cook for 1 minute.

Stir in the flour, then mix in the canned tomatoes and stock, add the bay leaves and a little salt and pepper, and bring to a boil. Transfer to the slow cooker pot and press the vegetables below the surface of the liquid. Cover with the lid and cook on high for 4–5 hours or until the root vegetables are tender.

Stir the goulash and discard the bay leaves. Spoon onto plates and top with spoonfuls of sour cream and a sprinkling of extra paprika, if desired. Serve with plain boiled rice.

For pork goulash, fry 1½ lb diced lean shoulder of pork in the oil until just beginning to brown. Add the onion and fry until both are lightly browned. Add the red pepper and 1 cup sliced mushrooms, then stir in the paprika, pepper flakes, and caraway seeds, omitting the root vegetables and celery. Continue as above, but cook on low for 8–10 hours.

beet & mascarpone risotto

Preparation time **20 minutes**
Cooking temperature **low**
Cooking time **1¾–2 hours**
Serves **4**

2 tablespoons **butter**
1 tablespoon **olive oil**
1 **red onion**, chopped
1 **garlic clove**, finely chopped
1¼ cups cooked, diced **beets**
1¼ cups **risotto rice**
⅔ cup **red wine**
4 cups **vegetable stock**
2 sprigs of **thyme**
salt and **pepper**

To serve
⅔ cup **mascarpone cheese**
4 teaspoons chopped **thyme leaves**
Parmesan cheese shavings

Preheat the slow cooker if necessary; see the manufacturer's instructions. Heat the butter and oil in a large skillet, add the onion, and fry, stirring, for 5 minutes or until softened.

Stir in the garlic, beets, and rice and cook for 1 minute, then mix in the wine and stock. Add the thyme and a little salt and pepper and bring to a boil, stirring.

Pour the mixture into the slow cooker pot. Cover with the lid and cook on low for 1¾–2 hours or until the rice is tender and almost all the stock has been absorbed.

Spoon into bowls and top with spoonfuls of mascarpone mixed with thyme, a little extra pepper, and a generous sprinkling of Parmesan shavings.

For mushroom & thyme risotto, soak ⅓ cup dried porcini mushrooms in ⅔ cup boiling water for 15 minutes. Fry the onion in butter and oil as above, then add the garlic, 8 oz mixed sliced mushrooms, and an extra 2 tablespoons butter and fry briefly. Omit the beets. Add the rice and cook for 1 minute, then add the soaked mushrooms and their soaking liquid, the red wine, stock, thyme, and salt and pepper and bring to a boil. Continue as above.

tomato & squash curry

Preparation time **20 minutes**
Cooking temperature **low**
Cooking time **5–6 hours**
Serves **4**

2 tablespoons **butter**
1 **onion**, chopped
½ **butternut squash**, about
   13 oz, peeled, seeded,
   and diced
2 **garlic cloves**, finely
   chopped
1½ inch **fresh ginger root**,
   peeled and finely chopped
½–1 mild **red chili**, to taste,
   seeded and finely chopped
4 tablespoons **korma curry
   paste**
⅔ cup **vegetable stock**
8 **plum tomatoes**, about
   1¼ lb in total, halved
2 oz **creamed coconut**,
   crumbled
salt and **pepper**
roughly chopped **cilantro**,
   to garnish

Preheat the slow cooker if necessary; see the manufacturer's instructions. Heat the butter in a large skillet, add the onion, and fry until softened.

Stir in the butternut squash, garlic, ginger, and chili and cook for 2–3 minutes. Mix in the curry paste and cook for 1 minute to release the curry flavor. Stir in the stock and bring to a boil.

Transfer the mixture to the slow cooker pot. Arrange the tomatoes, cut side uppermost, in a single layer on top of the squash, then sprinkle with the coconut and a little salt and pepper. Cover with the lid and cook on low for 5–6 hours or until the squash is tender and the tomatoes are soft but still holding their shape.

Spoon into bowls, sprinkle with roughly chopped cilantro, and serve with plain or pilau rice (see below) and naan bread.

For quick pilau rice to accompany the curry, rinse 1 cup basmati rice with cold water several times, then drain. Heat 1 tablespoon butter and 1 tablespoon sunflower oil in a large skillet, add 1 chopped onion and fry until softened. Stir in 1 dried red chili, 1 cinnamon stick, halved, 1 teaspoon cumin seeds, 1 bay leaf, 6 crushed cardamom pods, ½ teaspoon turmeric, and some salt. Pour on 2 cups boiling water, cover with a lid, and simmer gently for 10 minutes. Take off the heat and leave for 5–8 minutes—don't be tempted to lift the lid until ready to serve—then fluff up with a fork and spoon onto plates.

eggplants with baked eggs

Preparation time **20 minutes**
Cooking temperature **high**
Cooking time **2¾–3 hours**
   20 minutes
Serves **4**

4 tablespoons **olive oil**
1 **onion**, chopped
2 medium **eggplants**, cubed
2 **garlic cloves**, finely
   chopped
1 lb **tomatoes**, cut into large
   chunks
½ teaspoon **smoked paprika**
½ teaspoon **ground cumin**
½ teaspoon **ground cilantro**
½ cup **quinoa**
1¼ cups **vegetable stock**
¾ cup frozen **peas** (optional)
4 **eggs**
salt and **pepper**
chopped **mint**, to garnish

Preheat the slow cooker if necessary; see the manufacturer's instructions. Heat the oil in a large skillet, add the onion and eggplants, and fry, stirring, until the eggplants are golden.

Stir in the garlic, tomatoes, and spices and cook for 1 minute. Mix in the quinoa and stock, add a little salt and pepper, and bring to a boil. Transfer the mixture to the slow cooker pot. Cover with the lid and cook on high for 2½–3 hours.

Stir in the frozen peas, if using, and add a little boiling water if the quinoa has begun to stick around the edges of the pot. Make 4 dips with a spoon, then break and drop an egg into each dip. Cover and cook for 15–20 minutes or until the egg whites are set and the yolks still soft.

Spoon onto plates, sprinkle the eggs with a little extra salt and pepper, and garnish with chopped mint. Serve with toasted pita breads, cut into strips.

For eggplant ratatouille with baked eggs, omit the ground spices and quinoa and make up the recipe as above, adding 1 diced zucchini and 1 cored, seeded, and diced orange bell pepper with the garlic, tomatoes, and smoked paprika. Add ¾ cup vegetable stock, season with salt and pepper, and continue as above, omitting the peas. Serve sprinkled with torn basil leaves, spooned over toasted rustic-style bread.

pepperonata

Preparation time **20 minutes**
Cooking temperature **high**
Cooking time **3–4 hours**
Serves **3–4**

2 tablespoons **olive oil**
1 **onion**, chopped
3 **different colored bell peppers**, cored, seeded, and diced
2 **garlic cloves**, finely chopped
1 tablespoon **all-purpose flour**
13 oz can **chopped tomatoes**
1 teaspoon **superfine sugar**
2 sprigs of **basil**
⅔ cup **vegetable stock**
1 lb package chilled **gnocchi**
salt and **pepper**
basil leaves, to garnish
freshly grated **Parmesan cheese**, to serve

Preheat the slow cooker if necessary; see the manufacturer's instructions. Heat the oil in a large skillet, add the onion and fry, stirring until softened. Add the peppers and garlic and fry for 1–2 minutes.

Stir in the flour, mix in the tomatoes, then add the sugar, the basil, torn into pieces, stock, and a little salt and pepper. Bring to a boil, then pour into the slow cooker pot. Cover with the lid and cook on high for 3–4 hours or until the peppers are tender.

When almost ready to serve, bring a large saucepan of water to a boil, add the gnocchi, and cook for 2–3 minutes or until they float to the surface and are piping hot. Drain and gently stir into the pepperonata in the slow cooker pot. Spoon into shallow bowls and sprinkle with torn basil leaves and grated Parmesan.

For pepperonata & white bean stew, add a 13½ oz can drained navy beans to the stew when adding the tomatoes. Continue as above, omitting the gnocchi. Thickly slice and toast some ciabatta bread, rub the toast with a cut garlic clove, and drizzle with a little olive oil. Serve with the stew.

spiced date & chickpea pilaf

Preparation time **15 minutes**
Cooking temperature **low**
Cooking time **3–4 hours**
Serves **4**

1 tablespoon **olive oil**
1 **onion**, chopped
1–2 **garlic cloves**, finely
  chopped
1½ inches **fresh ginger root**,
  peeled and finely chopped
1 teaspoon **turmeric**
1 teaspoon **ground cumin**,
  plus extra to garnish
1 teaspoon **ground cilantro**
1 cup easy-cook **brown rice**
13½ oz can **chickpeas**,
  drained
½ cup ready-chopped pitted
  dates
4 cups **vegetable stock**
salt and **pepper**

Onion garnish
1 tablespoon **olive oil**
1 **onion**, thinly sliced
⅔ cup **whole milk yogurt**
chopped **cilantro**

Preheat the slow cooker if necessary; see the
manufacturer's instructions. Heat the oil in a large
skillet, add the onion and fry, stirring, for 5 minutes
or until softened and just beginning to turn golden.

Stir in the garlic, ginger, and ground spices and cook
for 1 minute. Add the rice, chickpeas, dates, stock, and
a little salt and pepper and bring to a boil, stirring. Pour
into the slow cooker pot, cover with the lid, and cook on
low for 3–4 hours or until the rice is tender and almost
all the stock has been absorbed.

Meanwhile, make the onion garnish. Heat the oil in a
skillet, add the sliced onion and fry over a medium heat,
stirring, until crisp and golden. Stir the pilaf, spoon into
bowls, and top with a spoonful of yogurt, a little extra
cumin, the onions, and a little chopped cilantro.

For chicken & almond pilaf, add 1 lb diced
boneless, skinless chicken thighs to the skillet with
the onion. Continue as above, omitting the dates. To
serve, replace the onion garnish with ½ cup slivered
almonds, fried in the oil until golden, and a little
chopped mint, if desired.

barley risotto with blue cheese

Preparation time **20 minutes**
Cooking temperature **low**
Cooking time **6¼–8¼ hours**
Serves **4**

1 cup **pearl barley**
1 **onion**, finely chopped
2 **garlic cloves**, finely
    chopped
1 lb **butternut squash**,
    peeled, seeded, and cut
    into ¾ inch pieces
4 cups boiling **vegetable
    stock**
2½ cups baby **spinach**,
    washed and well drained

Blue cheese butter
½ cup **butter**, at room
    temperature
4 oz **blue cheese** (rind
    removed)
1 **garlic clove**, finely chopped
¼ teaspoon **dried red pepper
    flakes**
salt and **pepper**

Preheat the slow cooker if necessary; see the manufacturer's instructions. Put the pearl barley, onion, garlic, and butternut squash into the slow cooker pot. Add the stock and a little salt and pepper. Cover with the lid and cook on low for 6–8 hours or until the barley and squash are tender.

Meanwhile, make the blue cheese butter. Put the butter on a plate, crumble the cheese on top, add the garlic and pepper flakes and mash together with a fork. Spoon the butter into a line on a piece of nonstick parchment paper, then wrap it in paper and roll it backward and forward to make a neat sausage shape. Chill in the refrigerator until required.

When almost ready to serve, stir the risotto, slice half the blue cheese butter and add to the slow cooker pot. Mix together until just beginning to melt, then add the spinach. Replace the lid and cook, still on low, for 15 minutes or until the spinach has just wilted. Ladle into shallow bowls and top with slices of the remaining butter.

For barley risotto with garlic & cilantro cream, make up the risotto as above, replacing the squash with 1 lb sweet potato and adding 2 cups sliced cup mushrooms with the stock. Cook as above, omitting the spinach and blue cheese butter. Mix together ¾ cup sour cream, 1 finely chopped garlic clove, 3 tablespoons finely chopped cilantro, and 3 chopped scallions. Ladle the risotto into bowls and top with spoonfuls of the cream.

cauliflower & spinach balti

Preparation time **10 minutes**
Cooking temperature **low**
Cooking time **5¼–6¼ hours**
Serves **4**

1 tablespoon **sunflower oil**
1 **onion**, chopped
2¼ cups canned **balti curry sauce**
1 large **cauliflower**, trimmed and cut into large pieces, about 1½ lb prepared weight
13½ oz can **green lentils**, drained
3 cups **spinach**, washed and torn into pieces

Preheat the slow cooker if necessary; see the manufacturer's instructions. Heat the oil in a large skillet, add the onion and fry, stirring, for 5 minutes or until softened. Add the curry sauce and bring to a boil.

Put the cauliflower and lentils into the slow cooker pot, then pour over the hot sauce. Cover with the lid and cook on low for 5–6 hours or until the cauliflower is tender.

Stir the cauliflower and lentil mixture and sprinkle the spinach on top. Replace the lid and cook, still on low, for 10–15 minutes or until the spinach has just wilted. Spoon into bowls and serve with warm naan bread.

For mushroom & sweet potato balti, make up the sauce as above. Replace the cauliflower with 12 oz quartered cup mushrooms and 12 oz diced sweet potatoes and put into the slow cooker pot with the lentils. Pour over the sauce, cover with the lid, and cook on low for 6–7 hours or until the sweet potatoes are tender. Add the spinach and cook and serve as above.

eggplant timbale

Preparation time **25 minutes**
Cooking temperature **high**
Cooking time **1½–2 hours**
Serves **2**

4 tablespoons **olive oil**, plus
  extra for greasing
1 large **eggplant**, thinly sliced
1 small **onion**, chopped
1 **garlic clove**, finely chopped
½ teaspoon **ground cinnamon**
¼ teaspoon grated **nutmeg**
3 tablespoons **pistachio nuts**,
  roughly chopped
3 tablespoons pitted **dates**,
  roughly chopped
3 tablespoons ready-to-eat
  dried **apricots**, roughly
  chopped
6 tablespoons easy-cook
  long-grain rice
1¼ cups boiling **vegetable
  stock**
salt and **pepper**

Preheat the slow cooker if necessary; see the manufacturer's instructions. Lightly oil the base of 2 soufflé dishes, each 1½ cups, and base-line each with a circle of nonstick parchment paper, checking first that they will fit in the slow cooker pot.

Heat 1 tablespoon of the oil in a large skillet, add one-third of the eggplants, and fry on both sides until softened and golden. Scoop out of the pan with a slotted spoon and transfer to a plate. Repeat with the rest of the eggplants, using 2 more tablespoons of oil.

Heat the remaining 1 tablespoon of oil in the pan, add the onion and fry for 5 minutes or until softened. Stir in the garlic, spices, nuts, fruit, and rice. Add a little salt and pepper and mix well.

Arrange one-third of the eggplant slices in the base of the 2 dishes, overlapping the slices. Spoon one-quarter of the rice mixture into each dish, add a second layer of eggplant slices, then divide the remaining rice equally between the dishes. Top with the remaining eggplant slices. Pour the stock into the dishes, cover with lightly oiled foil, and put in the slow cooker pot.

Pour boiling water into the pot to come halfway up the sides of the dishes. Cover with the lid and cook on high for 1½–2 hours or until the rice is tender. Lift the dishes out of the slow cooker pot using a dish towel and remove the foil. Loosen the edges of the timbales with a knife, turn out onto plates, and peel off the lining paper. Serve hot with a green salad or baked tomatoes.

balsamic tomatoes with spaghetti

Preparation time **10 minutes**
Cooking temperature **high**
Cooking time **3–4 hours**
Serves **4**

1 tablespoon **olive oil**, for greasing
1½ lb **plum tomatoes**, halved
4 tablespoons **white wine**
4 teaspoons good **balsamic vinegar**
12 oz **spaghetti**
salt and **pepper**
basil leaves, to garnish
freshly grated or shaved **Parmesan cheese**, to serve

Preheat the slow cooker if necessary; see the manufacturer's instructions. Brush the oil over the base of the slow cooker pot, add the tomatoes, cut side down, drizzle over the wine and vinegar, and add a little salt and pepper. Cover with the lid and cook on high for 3–4 hours or until the tomatoes are tender.

When almost ready to serve, bring a large saucepan of water to a boil, add the pasta, and cook for 6–7 minutes or until tender. Drain and mix into the sauce. Spoon the pasta into bowls and sprinkle with basil leaves and grated or shaved Parmesan.

For pesto baked tomatoes, oil the base of the slow cooker pot as above, sprinkling with 2 finely chopped garlic cloves before adding the tomatoes. Drizzle with the wine and 1 tablespoon pesto sauce, omitting the vinegar. Cook and serve as above.

herby stuffed peppers

Preparation time **20 minutes**
Cooking temperature **low**
Cooking time **4–5 hours**
Serves **4**

4 different colored bell peppers
½ cup easy-cook **brown rice**
13½ oz can **chickpeas**, drained
small bunch of **parsley**, roughly chopped
small bunch of **mint**, roughly chopped
1 **onion**, finely chopped
2 **garlic cloves**, finely chopped
½ teaspoon **smoked paprika**
1 teaspoon **ground allspice**
2½ cups boiling **vegetable stock**
salt and **pepper**

Preheat the slow cooker if necessary; see the manufacturer's instructions. Cut the top off each pepper, then remove the core and seeds.

Mix together the rice, chickpeas, herbs, onion, garlic, paprika, allspice, and plenty of salt and pepper in a bowl. Spoon the mixture into the peppers, then put the peppers into the slow cooker pot.

Pour the hot stock around the peppers, cover with the lid, and cook on low for 4–5 hours or until the rice and peppers are tender. Spoon into dishes and serve with salad and spoonfuls of whole milk yogurt flavored with extra chopped herbs, if desired.

For chilied stuffed peppers, fry the onion in 1 tablespoon olive oil until softened. Stir in the garlic and ½ teaspoon each of hot paprika or chili powder, ground allspice, ground cinnamon, and ground cumin. Mix with the brown rice and a drained 13½ oz can red kidney beans instead of the chickpeas. Spoon into the peppers and put into the slow cooker. Stir 2 tablespoons tomato paste into the stock and continue as above.

tarka dhal

Preparation time **15 minutes**
Cooking temperature **high**
Cooking time **3–4 hours**
Serves **4**

1¼ cups **red lentils**
1 **onion**, finely chopped
½ teaspoon **turmeric**
½ teaspoon **cumin seeds**,
  roughly crushed
¾ inch **fresh ginger root**,
  peeled and finely chopped
1 cup canned **chopped
  tomatoes**
2½ cups boiling **vegetable
  stock**
salt and **pepper**
cilantro leaves, to garnish
⅔ cup **plain yogurt**, to serve

Tarka
1 tablespoon **sunflower oil**
2 teaspoons **black mustard
  seeds**
½ teaspoon **cumin seeds**,
  roughly crushed
pinch of **turmeric**
2 **garlic cloves**, finely
  chopped

Preheat the slow cooker if necessary; see the manufacturer's instructions. Rinse the lentils well with cold water, drain, and put into the slow cooker pot with the onion, spices, ginger, tomatoes, and boiling stock. Stir in a little salt and pepper, cover with the lid, and cook on high for 3–4 hours or until the lentils are soft.

When almost ready to serve, make the tarka. Heat the oil in a small skillet, add the mustard and cumin seeds, turmeric, and garlic and fry, stirring, for 2 minutes. Roughly mash the lentil mixture and spoon it into bowls. Top with spoonfuls of yogurt and drizzle with the tarka. Garnish with torn cilantro leaves and serve with warm naan bread.

For spinach & egg tarka dhal, cook the lentils as above. Put 4 eggs in a pan of cold water, bring to a boil, and simmer for 8 minutes. Drain, peel, and halve the eggs. Twenty minutes before the end of the lentil cooking time, add the eggs to the slow cooker pot with 4½ cups finely shredded spinach and press below the surface of the sauce. Replace the lid and continue cooking. Serve with the tarka, yogurt, and cilantro as above.

food for
friends

salmon-wrapped cod with leeks

Preparation time **30 minutes**
Cooking temperature **low**
Cooking time **1½–2 hours**
Serves **4**

2 **cod loins**, about 1½ lb
    in total
juice of 1 **lemon**
4 sprigs of **dill weed**, plus
    extra to garnish (optional)
4 slices of **smoked salmon**,
    about 6 oz in total
1 **leek**, thinly sliced; white and
    green parts kept separate
4 tablespoons **Noilly Prat**
¾ cup boiling **fish stock**
2 teaspoons drained **capers**
    (optional)
⅓ cup **butter**, diced
2 tablespoons chopped
    chives or **parsley**
salt and **pepper**

Preheat the slow cooker if necessary; see the manufacturer's instructions. Cut each cod loin in half to give 4 portions, then drizzle with the lemon juice and sprinkle with salt and pepper. Add a dill sprig to the top of each portion, then wrap with a slice of smoked salmon.

Put the white leek slices into the base of the slow cooker pot, arrange the fish on top in a single layer, tilting them slightly at an angle, if needed, to make them fit. Add the Noilly Prat and hot stock, then cover and cook on low for 1½–2 hours or until the fish flakes easily when pressed in the center with a knife.

Lift out the fish with a spatula and put it on a serving plate, cover with foil, and keep hot. Pour the white leeks and cooking juices from the slow cooker pot into a saucepan, add the reserved green leek slices and the capers, if using, and boil rapidly for about 5 minutes or until the liquid is reduced to 4–6 tablespoons. Scoop out and reserve the leeks as soon as the green slices have softened.

Whisk in the butter, a piece at a time until melted, and continue until all the butter has been added and the sauce is smooth and glossy. Return the cooked leeks to the sauce with the chopped herbs and taste and adjust the seasoning. Arrange the fish on plates, then spoon the sauce around. Sprinkle with extra dill, if desired, and serve with baby new potatoes.

For smoked cod with buttered leeks, make up the recipe as above, with smoked cod loins, omitting the smoked salmon and dill and replacing the Noilly Prat with dry white wine.

venison puff pie

Preparation time **35 minutes**
Cooking temperature **low**
Cooking time **8–10 hours**
Serves 4–5

2 tablespoons **butter**
1 tablespoon **olive oil**, plus
   extra for greasing
1½ lb **venison**, diced
1 **onion**, chopped
2 tablespoons **all-purpose**
   flour
¾ cup **red wine**
1 cup **lamb** or **beef stock**
3 medium raw **beets**, peeled
   and cut into ½ inch dice
1 tablespoon **red currant jelly**
1 tablespoon **tomato paste**
10 **juniper berries**, roughly
   crushed
3 sprigs of **thyme**
1 **bay leaf**
1 sheet, about 7 oz, ready-
   rolled **puff pastry**
beaten **egg**, for glazing
salt and **pepper**

Preheat the slow cooker if necessary; see the manufacturer's instructions. Heat the butter and oil in a large skillet, add the venison a few pieces at a time until all the pieces are in the pan, then fry, stirring, until evenly browned. Scoop the venison out of the pan with a slotted spoon and transfer to the slow cooker pot. Add the onion to the pan and fry for 5 minutes until softened.

Stir in the flour, then mix in the wine and stock. Add the beets, red currant jelly, and tomato paste, then the juniper, 2 sprigs of thyme, and the bay leaf. Season with salt and pepper and bring to a boil. Pour the sauce over the venison, cover with the lid, and cook on low for 8–10 hours or until tender.

When you are almost ready to serve, preheat the oven to 425°F. Unroll the pastry and trim the edges to make an oval similar in size to the slow cooker pot. Transfer to an oiled baking sheet, flute the edges and add leaves from the trimmings. Brush with egg, sprinkle with the remaining thyme leaves stripped from the stem and coarse salt, and bake in the preheated oven for about 20 minutes until well risen and golden.

Stir the venison and spoon onto plates. Cut the pastry into wedges and place on top of the venison. Serve with roasted parsnips and baby carrots.

For lamb & mushroom puff pie, replace the venison with 1½ lb diced shoulder or leg of lamb and fry as above. Fry the onion, then add 8 oz quartered cup mushrooms in place of the beets and fry for 2–3 minutes. Stir in the flour and continue as above.

creamy chicken korma

Preparation time **15 minutes**
Cooking temperature **low**
Cooking time **6¼–7¼ hours**
Serves **4**

2 tablespoons **butter**
4 boneless, skinless **chicken breasts**, about 5 oz each
1 **onion**, finely chopped
2 **garlic cloves**, finely chopped
1 inch **fresh ginger root**, peeled and finely chopped
3 tablespoons **korma curry paste**
4 tablespoons **ground almonds**
¾ cup **chicken stock**
3 tablespoons **heavy cream**
3 tablespoons chopped **cilantro**
salt and **pepper**
3 tablespoons toasted **slivered almonds**, to garnish

Preheat the slow cooker if necessary; see the manufacturer's instructions. Heat the butter in a large skillet, add the chicken and fry on both sides until browned but not cooked through. Lift out of the pan with a slotted spoon and transfer to the slow cooker pot.

Add the onion, garlic, and ginger to the pan and fry for 2–3 minutes, then stir in the curry paste and cook for 1 minute. Stir in the ground almonds, stock and salt and pepper and bring to a boil.

Pour the sauce over the chicken. Cover with the lid and cook on low for 6–7 hours or until the chicken is cooked through.

Stir in the cream and chopped cilantro, replace the lid, and cook, still on low, for 15 minutes. Slice the chicken. Spoon onto rice-lined plates and sprinkle with the almonds.

For creamy paneer korma, omit the chicken and fry 2 small very finely chopped onions in 2 tablespoons butter until softened. Add the garlic, ginger, and curry paste, then stir in the ground almonds and stock and bring to a boil as above. Drain and cut 1 lb paneer (Indian cheese) into ¾ inch cubes and add to the slow cooker pot with the sauce. Continue as above.

braised duck with orange sauce

Preparation time **15 minutes**
Cooking temperature **high**
Cooking time **4–5 hours**
Serves **4**

4 **duck legs**, about 6 oz each
1 **onion**, sliced
2 tablespoons **all-purpose flour**
⅔ cup **chicken stock**
⅔ cup **dry white wine**
1 large **orange**, half sliced, half squeezed juice
1 **bay leaf**
1 teaspoon **Dijon mustard**
salt
½ teaspoon **black peppercorns**, roughly crushed

Preheat the slow cooker if necessary; see the manufacturer's instructions. Dry-fry the duck in a large skillet over a low heat until the fat begins to run, then increase the heat until the duck is browned on both sides. Lift out of the pan with a slotted spoon and transfer to the slow cooker pot.

Pour off any excess fat to leave about 1 tablespoon. Fry the onions until softened. Stir in the flour, then mix in the stock, wine, orange juice, bay leaf, a little salt, and the crushed peppercorns and bring to a boil, stirring. Add the sliced orange.

Pour the sauce over the duck, cover with the lid, and cook on high for 4–5 hours or until the duck is tender and almost falling off the bones. Serve with rice and steamed green beans.

For braised duck with cranberries & port, fry the duck and onions as above. Mix in the flour and stock, then replace the wine with ⅔ cup ruby port and 1 cup fresh cranberries. Add orange slices and juice and continue as above.

chilied beef with chocolate

Preparation time **15 minutes**
Cooking temperature **low**
Cooking time **8–10 hours**
Serves **4**

1 tablespoon **sunflower oil**
1 lb **ground beef**
1 **onion**, chopped
3 **garlic cloves**, finely
   chopped
1 teaspoon **ground cinnamon**
1 teaspoon **ground cumin**
½–1 teaspoon **smoked or hot**
   paprika, plus extra to
   garnish
¼–½ teaspoon **dried red**
   pepper flakes
1 **bay leaf**
13 oz can **chopped tomatoes**
13½ oz can **red kidney beans**,
   drained
2 tablespoons **dark brown**
   sugar
1¼ cups **beef stock**
1 oz **bittersweet chocolate**
salt and **pepper**
sour cream, to serve

Preheat the slow cooker if necessary; see the manufacturer's instructions. Heat the oil in a skillet, add the beef and onion, and fry, stirring, until the meat is evenly browned.

Stir in the garlic, ground spices, and bay leaf and cook for 1 minute. Mix in the tomatoes, beans, sugar, and stock, then add the chocolate and a little salt and pepper and bring to a boil, stirring.

Pour into the slow cooker pot, cover with the lid, and cook on low for 8–10 hours or until cooked through. Stir, spoon onto plates, and top with a little sour cream, salsa (see below), and extra paprika. Serve with rice.

For avocado & red onion salsa to accompany the chilied beef, halve 1 large ripe avocado, remove the pit and peel away the skin. Dice the flesh, then toss in the grated zest and juice of 2 limes. Mix with 1 small finely chopped red onion, 1 chopped tomato, and a small bunch of chopped cilantro.

trout spirals with lemon foam

Preparation time **30 minutes**
Cooking temperature **low**
Cooking time **1½–2 hours**
Serves **4**

¼ cup **butter**, at room
   temperature
grated zest and juice of
   1 **lemon**
4 **trout fillets**, skinned, about
   1 lb 5 oz in total
1 **plaice**, filleted into 4,
   skinned
¾ cup boiling **fish stock**
3 **egg yolks**
salt and **pepper**

Preheat the slow cooker if necessary; see the manufacturer's instructions. Beat the butter with the lemon zest and a little salt and pepper.

Lay the trout fillets on a cutting board so that the skinned sides are uppermost. Trim the edges to neaten, if needed, and spread with half the lemon butter. Top with the plaice fillets, skinned side uppermost, and spread with the remaining butter. Roll up each fish stack, starting at the tapered end. Secure each spiral with 2 toothpicks at right angles to each other and arrange in the base of the slow cooker pot.

Pour the lemon juice and boiling stock over the fish and add a little salt and pepper. Cover with the lid and cook on low for 1½–2 hours or until the fish flakes easily when pressed in the center with a knife.

Lift the fish spirals out of the slow cooker pot with a slotted spoon, put onto a serving plate, and remove the toothpicks. Strain the cooking juices into a bowl. Put the egg yolks in a saucepan and gradually whisk in the strained stock until smooth. Cook over a medium heat, whisking constantly without boiling for 3–4 minutes or until lightly thickened and foamy. Pour into a pitcher. Serve the fish with a generous of the sauce around each one, salad, and a separate bowl of new potatoes.

For salmon steaks with lemon & tarragon foam, put 4 salmon steaks, about 5 oz each and spread with the lemon butter, in the base of the slow cooker pot and continue as above. Make up the sauce as above, then whisk in 2 teaspoons chopped tarragon just before serving.

new orleans chicken gumbo

Preparation time **20 minutes**

Cooking temperature **low and high**

Cooking time **8¼–10¼ hours**

Serves **4**

2 tablespoons **olive oil**

1 lb boneless, skinless **chicken thighs**, cubed

3 oz ready-diced **chorizo**

3 oz **smoked bacon**, diced

1 **onion**, sliced

2 **garlic cloves**, chopped

2 tablespoons **all-purpose flour**

2½ cups **chicken stock**

2 **bay leaves**

2 sprigs of **thyme**

salt

¼–½ teaspoon **cayenne pepper**, to taste

3 **celery sticks**, sliced

½ each of 3 different colored **bell peppers**, cored, seeded, and sliced

4 oz **okra**, thickly sliced (optional)

chopped **parsley**, to garnish

Preheat the slow cooker if necessary; see the manufacturer's instructions. Heat the oil in a large skillet, add the chicken a few pieces at time until all the pieces are in the pan, then add the chorizo and bacon and fry, stirring, until the chicken is golden. Lift out of the pan with a slotted spoon and transfer to the slow cooker.

Add the onion to the skillet and fry until softened. Mix in the garlic, then stir in the flour. Gradually mix in the stock, add the herbs and a little salt and cayenne to taste. Bring to a boil, stirring.

Mix the celery and different colored peppers into the chicken, then pour over the hot onion mixture. Cover with the lid and cook on low for 8–10 hours or until the chicken is cooked through.

When almost ready to serve, stir the okra into the chicken gumbo, if using. Replace the lid and cook on high for 15 minutes or until the okra has just softened. Stir once more, then sprinkle with chopped parsley. Ladle into shallow rice-lined bowls and serve with a soup spoon and fork.

For crab gumbo soup, omit the chicken and make up the gumbo as above, replacing the chicken stock with 2½ cups fish stock and adding 2 sliced carrots, 2 diced sweet potatoes, and 1 diced zucchini to the slow cooker pot with the celery and peppers. Add 7 oz cooked jumbo shrimp, thawed if frozen, rinsed with cold water and drained, and 7 oz drained canned white crabmeat to the pot with the okra, if using, and cook on high for 20–30 minutes or until the fish is piping hot. Serve with rice.

tamarind beef with ginger beer

Preparation time **20 minutes**
Cooking temperature **low**
Cooking time **8–10 hours**
Serves **4**

2 tablespoons **sunflower oil**
1½ lb lean **stewing beef**, cubed
1 **onion**, chopped
2 **garlic cloves**, finely chopped
2 tablespoons **all-purpose flour**
1½ cups **ginger beer**
6 teaspoons **tamarind paste**
½ teaspoon **dried red pepper flakes**
1 teaspoon **ground mixed spice**
1 tablespoon **dark brown sugar**
salt and **pepper**

Preheat the slow cooker if necessary; see the manufacturer's instructions. Heat the oil in a large skillet, add the beef a few pieces at a time until all the pieces are in the pan, then add the onion and fry over a medium heat, stirring, until the meat is evenly browned.

Stir in the garlic and flour. Gradually mix in the ginger beer, then stir in the tamarind paste, dried pepper flakes and spice, sugar, and a little salt and pepper and bring to a boil, stirring.

Transfer to the slow cooker pot and press the beef below the surface of the liquid. Cover with the lid and cook on low for 8–10 hours or until the meat is cooked through and tender.

Stir the beef, then ladle into bowls and top with garlic and cilantro croutes (see below) and serve with steamed broccoli.

For ginger & cilantro croutes to accompany the casserole, beat ¾ inch piece peeled and grated ginger root with 2 finely chopped garlic cloves and ¼ cup butter, stir in ½ mild, seeded, finely chopped red chili, or a large pinch of dried red pepper flakes, 3 tablespoons chopped cilantro leaves, and a little salt and pepper. Toast 8 slices of French bread on both sides and spread with the butter while hot. Arrange the croutes on top of the casserole and serve immediately.

fish pie

Preparation time **20 minutes**
Cooking temperature **low**
Cooking time **2–3 hours**
Serves **4–5**

1 tablespoon **sunflower oil**
1 **leek**, trimmed, cleaned, and
 thinly sliced
¼ cup **butter**
½ cup **all-purpose flour**
1¾ cups **ultrapasteurized
 milk**
⅔ cup **fish stock**
¾ cup grated **cheddar cheese**
1 **bay leaf**
1 lb 10 oz mixed **salmon**, and
 smoked and **unsmoked
 haddock**, skinned and cut
 into large cubes
salt and **pepper**

Topping
4 tablespoons chopped
 parsley
1 lb 10 oz hot homemade or
 bought **mashed potato**
2 tablespoons **butter**
3 tablespoons grated **cheddar
 cheese**

Preheat the slow cooker if necessary; see the manufacturer's instructions. Heat the oil in a saucepan, add the leek and fry, stirring, for 4–5 minutes or until softened. Scoop out of the pan with a slotted spoon and transfer to a plate.

Add the butter, flour, and milk to the pan and bring to a boil, whisking constantly until thickened and smooth. Mix in the stock, cheese, bay leaf, and a little salt and pepper.

Arrange the cubed fish in the slow cooker pot so that it is an even layer, then pour over the hot sauce. Cover with the lid and cook on low for 2–3 hours or until the fish flakes easily when pressed in the center with a knife.

When almost ready to serve, stir the parsley into the hot mashed potatoes. Stir the fish, spoon into individual ovenproof dishes, if desired. Spoon the potatoes over the top, dot with the butter, and sprinkle with the cheese. Lift the pot out of the housing using oven mitts if not using separate dishes and brown under the broiler until golden. Serve with steamed asparagus.

For mixed fish & spinach gratin, wash 13 oz baby spinach leaves in cold water, drain, and place in a large saucepan. Cover and cook until just wilted. Transfer to a strainer and squeeze out as much water as possible. Spoon into the base of a 2 inch deep dish. Make up the fish pie mixture as above and spoon out of the slow cooker pot onto the spinach, then sprinkle with ½ cup grated cheddar and 4 tablespoons fresh bread crumbs. Broil as above.

prune stuffed pork tenderloin

Preparation time **40 minutes**
Cooking temperature **high**
Cooking time **3½–4 hours**
Serves **4**

2 **pork tenderloins**, just under
    13 oz each
1 slice of **bread**, crusts
    removed
1 small **onion**, quartered
2 **garlic cloves**, halved
1½ inches **fresh ginger root**,
    peeled and sliced
¼ teaspoon **ground allspice**
10 ready-to-eat pitted **prunes**
4 **bacon slices**
1 tablespoon **olive oil**
12 **shallots**, halved if large
2 tablespoons **cornstarch**
¾ cup **red wine**
1¼ cups **chicken stock**
1 tablespoon **tomato paste**
salt and **pepper**

Preheat the slow cooker if necessary; see the manufacturer's instructions. Trim the thinnest end off each pork tenderloin so each is 9 inches long, reserving the trimmings. Make a slit along the length of each and open out flat.

Put the pork trimmings into a food processor with the bread, onion, garlic, ginger, spice, and salt and pepper and mix until finely chopped. Spoon half the mixture along the length of one piece of pork, press the prunes on top, then cover with the rest of the stuffing and the remaining tenderloin. Season, then wrap the bacon around the pork and tie in place with twine.

Heat the oil in a large skillet, add the pork and shallots and fry, turning the pork until golden all over. Transfer to the slow cooker pot. Make a smooth paste with the cornstarch and a little cold water, then add to the pan with the remaining ingredients. Bring to a boil, stirring until thickened, then pour over the pork.

Cover with the lid and cook on high for 3½–4 hours or until the pork is cooked through and tender. Transfer the pork to a serving plate. Serve cut into thick slices, with the shallots and sauce, accompanied with steamed asparagus and creamy potato dauphinoise.

For apricot & pistachio stuffed pork tenderloin, slit the tenderloins as above. Replace the prunes with ¼ cup roughly chopped pistachio nuts, grated zest of ½ orange, and ½ cup ready-to-eat dried apricots, chopped, and add to the pork trimmings mixture and continue as above. To make the sauce, replace the red wine with ¾ cup hard cider.

beef & guinness puff pie

Preparation time **40 minutes**
Cooking temperature **low**
Cooking time **8–10 hours**
Serves **4–5**

2 tablespoons **sunflower oil**,
  plus extra for greasing
1½ lb lean **stewing beef**,
  cubed
1 **onion**, chopped
2 tablespoons **all-purpose
  flour**, plus extra for dusting
1¼ cups **Guinness**
⅔ cups **beef stock**
2 teaspoons **hot horseradish**
1 tablespoon **tomato paste**
1 **bay leaf**
2 cups sliced **cup
  mushrooms**
salt and **pepper**

Pastry
1 lb **puff pastry**, thawed
  if frozen
beaten **egg**, to glaze
4 oz **Stilton cheese** (rind
  removed), crumbled

Preheat the slow cooker if necessary; see the manufacturer's instructions. Heat the oil in a large skillet, add the meat a few pieces at a time until all the pieces are in the pan, then add the onion and fry over a medium heat, stirring until the meat is evenly browned.

Stir in the flour, then gradually mix in the Guinness and the stock. Stir in the horseradish, tomato paste, and a little salt and pepper, then add the bay leaf and bring to a boil. Transfer to the slow cooker pot and press the meat below the surface of the liquid. Cover with the lid and cook on low for 8–10 hours or until the meat is cooked through and very tender.

When almost ready to serve, preheat the oven to 400°F. Discard the bay leaf and divide the beef mixture between 4 pie dishes, each about 1¾ cups. Mix in the mushrooms, then brush the top edge of the dishes with a little egg. Cut the pastry into 4 and roll each piece out on a floured surface until a little larger than the dishes, then press onto the dishes. Trim off the excess pastry and crimp the edges. Mark diagonal lines on top and brush with beaten egg. Put on an oiled baking sheet and cook in the preheated oven for 30 minutes or until golden. Sprinkle with the Stilton and allow to melt for 1–2 minutes. Serve with green beans and curly kale.

For beery beef hotpot, make up the meat base as above, omitting the mushrooms and adding 2 diced carrots. Spoon into the slow cooker pot, then cover with 1 lb 6 oz thinly sliced potatoes, pressing them just below the stock. Cook as above. Dot 2 tablespoons butter over the potatoes, lift the pot out of the housing using oven mitts and brown under a hot broiler.

slow-cooked lamb shanks

Preparation time **20 minutes**
Cooking temperature **high**
Cooking time **5–7 hours**
Serves **4**

2 tablespoons **olive oil**
4 **lamb shanks**, about 12 oz
  each
1¼ lb **new potatoes**, thickly
  sliced
2 **onions**, sliced
3–4 **garlic cloves**, finely
  chopped
1¼ cups **white wine**
⅔ cup **lamb stock**
1 tablespoon **runny honey**
1 teaspoon **dried oregano**
1 **preserved lemon**, cut into
  chunks
½ cup **green olives** (optional)
salt and **pepper**
chopped **parsley**, to garnish

Preheat the slow cooker if necessary; see the manufacturer's instructions. Heat the oil in a large skillet, add the lamb and fry, turning until browned on all sides. Arrange the potatoes in the base of the slow cooker pot, then put the lamb on top.

Add the onion to the pan and fry until softened, then mix in the garlic. Add the wine, stock, honey, oregano, and a little salt and pepper and bring to a boil. Pour over the lamb, then add the lemons and olives, if using.

Cover with the lid and cook on high for 5–7 hours or until the potatoes are tender and the lamb is almost falling off the bone. Spoon into shallow bowls and sprinkle with parsley. Serve with a green salad.

For slow-cooked lamb shanks with prunes, fry the lamb as above and add to the potatoes. Fry the onion and garlic with 3 diced bacon slices, then mix in 300 ml 1¼ cups red wine, ⅔ cup lamb stock, 1 tablespoon tomato paste, ½ cup pitted prunes, a small bunch of mixed herbs, and salt and pepper. Cover and cook as above.

salmon & asparagus risotto

Preparation time **15 minutes**
Cooking temperature **low**
Cooking time **1¾–2 hours**
Serves **4**

2 tablespoons **butter**
1 tablespoon **olive oil**
1 **onion**, chopped
grated zest of **1 lemon**
1 cup **risotto rice**
⅔ cup **dry white wine**
3¾ cups **fish** or **vegetable stock**
4 **salmon steaks**, about 5 oz each
1 bunch of **asparagus**, trimmed and thickly sliced
salt and **pepper**
½ cup **sour cream**, to serve
chopped **chives**, to garnish

Preheat the slow cooker if necessary; see the manufacturer's instructions. Heat the butter and oil in a large skillet, add the onion and fry for 5 minutes or until softened. Stir in the lemon zest and rice and cook for 1 minute. Mix in the wine, stock, and a little salt and pepper and bring to a boil, stirring.

Pour into the slow cooker pot. Arrange the salmon steaks in a single layer on the rice, turning on their sides, if needed, so they are just below the surface of the stock. Cover with the lid and cook on low for 1¾–2 hours or until the rice is tender and the salmon flakes into opaque pieces when pressed in the center with a knife.

When almost ready to serve, bring a saucepan of water to a boil, add the asparagus, and cook for 5 minutes or until just tender. Spoon the rice into shallow bowls and top with spoonfuls of sour cream, the drained asparagus, and salmon steaks broken into pieces. Sprinkle with chopped chives and a little extra pepper.

For smoked fish kedgeree, add ½ teaspoon turmeric and 1 bay leaf to the fried onion instead of the lemon zest. Add 4 cups of stock, bring to a boil, then transfer to the slow cooker pot. Replace the salmon with 1¼ lb smoked haddock, cut into 2 pieces, then cook as above. Skin and flake the fish, discard the bay leaf, then return to the pot and stir in 4 tablespoons heavy cream and ½ cup just cooked frozen peas. Spoon into bowls and top with 4 hard-cooked eggs cut into wedges. Sprinkle with chopped chives and a little extra black pepper.

desserts

mini banana & date puddings

Preparation time **20 minutes**
Cooking temperature **high**
Cooking time **2–3 hours**
Serves **4**

½ cup **butter**, at room
    temperature, plus extra
    for greasing
½ cup **light brown sugar**
2 **eggs**, beaten
1 cup **self-rising flour**
1 small ripe **banana**, mashed
½ cup ready-chopped pitted
    dates
1 cup **ready-made toffee
    sauce**
2 oz **bittersweet chocolate**,
    broken into pieces

Preheat the slow cooker if necessary; see the manufacturer's instructions. Butter 4 metal pudding molds, each 1 cup, and base-line each with a circle of nonstick parchment paper, checking first that they will fit in the slow cooker pot.

Beat the butter and sugar in a bowl with a wooden spoon or hand-held electric mixer until soft and creamy. Gradually add alternate spoonfuls of egg and flour until both have all been added and the batter is smooth. Mash the banana on a plate, then beat into the pudding mix. Stir in the dates, then divide between the molds.

Cover each one with a square of foil and stand in the slow cooker pot. Pour boiling water into the pot to come halfway up the sides of the molds. Cover with the lid and cook on high for 2–3 hours or until the tops of the puddings spring back when pressed with a fingertip.

Lift the molds from the slow cooker pot using a dish towel and remove the foil. Loosen the edges with a knife and turn out onto plates. Pour the toffee sauce into a small saucepan, add the chocolate and warm through, stirring until the chocolate has just melted. Drizzle over the puddings and serve immediately.

For mini chocolate & banana puddings, make up the puddings with the butter, sugar, and eggs as above. Substitute 2 tablespoons cocoa for 2 tablespoons flour, then add with the remaining flour, mashed banana, and dates. Cook as above. Warm 4 tablespoons chocolate and hazelnut spread with 2 tablespoons heavy cream and 2 tablespoons milk in a saucepan, stir until smooth and serve with the puddings.

cider poached apples with granola

Preparation time **10 minutes**
Cooking temperature **high**
Cooking time **1½–2 hours**
Serves **4**

4 medium **cooking apples**,
    about 1½ lb in total, peeled,
    cored, and quartered
grated zest and juice of
    1 lemon
⅓ cup **golden raisins**
4 tablespoons **light brown
    sugar**
1 cup **hard cider**
1 tablespoon **butter**

Almond granola
2 tablespoons **butter**
1½ cups **granola-style cereal**
2 tablespoons **slivered
    almonds**
2 tablespoons **light brown
    sugar**

Preheat the slow cooker if necessary; see the manufacturer's instructions. Cut each apple quarter in half again, then put into the slow cooker and toss with the lemon zest and juice. Arrange the apples so that they are in a single layer.

Sprinkle with the golden raisins and sugar, pour over the cider, and dot with the butter. Cover with the lid and cook on high for 1½–2 hours or until the apples are tender but still holding their shape.

When almost ready to serve, heat the butter for the almond granola in a skillet, add the remaining ingredients and fry, stirring until hot and browned. Spoon the apples and the cidery juices into bowls and sprinkle hot granola on top. Serve with cream or ice cream.

For spiced poached apples with orange, arrange the apples in the slow cooker pot as above, adding the zest of 1 orange with the lemon juice and zest. Replace the golden raisins with 1 orange, peeled and cut into segments, 1 cinnamon stick, broken into pieces, and 4 cloves and sprinkle over the apples with the sugar. Pour over ½ cup apple juice and ½ cup water instead of the cider and dot with butter. Continue as above. Serve with scoops of vanilla ice cream.

jelly roly-poly pudding

Preparation time **25 minutes**
Cooking temperature **high**
Cooking time **3½–4 hours**
Serves **4**

2½ cups **self-rising flour**
1 scant cup **vegetable suet**
¼ cup **superfine sugar**
grated zest of 2 **lemons**
¾–1 cup **milk** or **milk** and
   water mixed
4 tablespoons **strawberry jelly**
salt

Preheat the slow cooker if necessary; see the manufacturer's instructions. Put the flour, suet, sugar, lemon zest, and a pinch of salt in a bowl and mix well. Gradually stir in the milk or milk and water to make a soft but not sticky dough. Knead lightly, then roll out on a piece of floured nonstick parchment paper to a rectangle about 9 x 12 inches. Turn the paper so that the shorter edges are facing you.

Spread the jelly over the pastry, leaving ¾ inch around the edges. Roll up, starting at a shorter edge, using the paper to help. Wrap in the paper, then in a sheet of foil. Twist the ends together tightly, leaving space for the pudding to rise.

Transfer the pudding to the slow cooker pot and raise off the base by standing it on 2 ramekin dishes. Pour boiling water into the pot to come a little up the sides of the pudding, being careful that the water cannot seep through any joins. Cover with the lid and cook on high for 3½–4 hours or until the pudding is light and fluffy. Lift out of the pot, then unwrap and cut into thick slices. Serve with hot custard.

For spotted dick, grate the zest of 1 large orange and reserve, squeeze the juice into a saucepan, bring to a boil, add 1 cup golden raisins, and allow to soak for 30 minutes. Make up the pastry as above, adding the orange zest, the grated zest of 1 lemon, and the soaked raisins before mixing with enough milk to make a soft dough. Shape into a log 9 inches long. Wrap in nonstick parchment paper and foil, then cook as above.

chocolate & coffee custard creams

Preparation time **20 minutes**,
  plus chilling
Cooking temperature **low**
Cooking time **3–3½ hours**
Serves **4**

1¾ cups **milk**
4 oz **bittersweet chocolate**,
  broken into pieces
1 teaspoon **instant coffee**
2 **eggs**
2 **egg yolks**
3 tablespoons **light brown
  sugar**
½ teaspoon **vanilla extract**
sifted **unsweetened cocoa
  powder**, to decorate

Topping
½ cup **heavy cream**
2 tablespoons **light brown
  sugar**
½ teaspoon **vanilla extract**

Preheat the slow cooker if necessary; see the manufacturer's instructions. Pour the milk into a saucepan and bring just to a boil. Remove from the heat, add the chocolate pieces and instant coffee, and set aside for 5 minutes, stirring occasionally, until the chocolate has melted.

Put the whole eggs, egg yolks, sugar, and vanilla extract in a bowl and whisk until just mixed. Gradually whisk in the hot chocolate milk until smooth. Strain through a strainer into the pan, then pour into 4 tall heatproof mugs, each 1 cup capacity, checking first that they will fit in the slow cooker pot.

Cover the tops of the mugs with foil and stand them in the slow cooker pot. Pour boiling water into the pot to come halfway up the sides of the mugs. Cover with the lid and cook on low for 3–3½ hours or until the custards are set and the tops can be lightly pressed with a fingertip.

Lift the mugs carefully out of the slow cooker pot using a dish towel. Allow to cool, then transfer to the refrigerator for at least 4 hours until chilled. Just before serving, whip the cream with the sugar and vanilla until soft swirls form. Spoon the topping over the custards and lightly dust with cocoa powder. Serve with dainty cookies.

For vanilla custard pots, bring the milk just to a boil as above. Whisk the whole eggs and egg yolks with 2 tablespoons superfine sugar and 1 teaspoon vanilla extract. Gradually whisk in the hot milk, then strain and continue as above, sprinkling the tops with a little grated nutmeg before cooking, if desired.

topsy turvy plum pudding

Preparation time **25 minutes**
Cooking temperature **high**
Cooking time **4–5 hours**
Serves **6**

½ cup **butter**, at room
temperature, plus extra
for greasing
1 cup **blackberries**, thawed
if frozen
7 oz ripe **red plums**, halved,
pitted, and sliced
2 tablespoons **red berry jelly**
½ cup **superfine sugar**
1 cup **self-rising flour**
2 **eggs**, beaten
⅓ cup **ground almonds**
few drops of **almond extract**
toasted **slivered almonds**, to
decorate (optional)

Preheat the slow cooker if necessary; see the
manufacturer's instructions. Lightly butter a 5 cup
soufflé dish and base-line with a circle of nonstick
parchment paper, checking first that the dish will fit
in the slow cooker pot. Arrange the blackberries and
plums in the base, then dot with the jelly.

Beat the butter and sugar in a bowl with a wooden
spoon or hand-held electric mixer until soft and creamy.
Gradually mix in alternate spoonfuls of flour and beaten
egg, and continue adding and beating until the batter is
smooth. Stir in the almonds and almond extract. Spoon
the batter over the fruit, spread it level, and cover the
top with foil.

Lower the dish into the slow cooker pot and pour
boiling water into the pot to come halfway up the sides
of the dish. Cover with the lid and cook on high for
4–5 hours or until the pudding is well risen and springs
back when pressed with a fingertip.

Lift the dish out of the slow cooker pot using a dish
towel and remove the foil. Loosen the edges of the
pudding with a knife and turn out onto a plate with a
rim. Decorate with toasted slivered almonds, if desired,
and serve hot with custard.

For peach & chocolate pudding, arrange 2 (or 1
if very large) halved, pitted, and sliced ripe peaches
in the base of the dish and dot with 2 tablespoons
apricot jelly. Make up the pudding mixture as above,
adding ¼ cup unsweetened cocoa powder and an
extra ¼ cup self-rising flour instead of the ground
almonds and almond extract. Continue as above.

hot chocolate mousses

Preparation time **25 minutes**
Cooking temperature **high**
Cooking time **1–1¼ hours**
Serves **4**

7 oz **bittersweet chocolate**,
  broken into pieces
¼ cup **butter**, plus extra
  for greasing
4 **eggs**, separated
4 tablespoons **superfine sugar**
1 tablespoon **warm water**
sifted **confectioners' sugar**, to
  decorate

Mint cream
6 tablespoons **heavy cream**
4 teaspoons chopped **mint**

Preheat the slow cooker if necessary; see the manufacturer's instructions. Put the chocolate and butter in a bowl, set over a saucepan of very gently simmering water making sure that the water does not touch the base of the bowl and leave until just melted.

Meanwhile, butter 4 mugs, each 1 cup, checking first that they will fit in the slow cooker pot.

Whisk the egg whites in a bowl until soft peaks, then gradually whisk in the sugar a teaspoonful at a time until it has all been added and the meringue is thick and glossy. Take the bowl of chocolate off the saucepan, stir in the egg yolks and warm water, and gently fold in a spoonful of the egg whites to loosen the mixture. Fold in the remaining egg whites, then divide between the mugs.

Cover the tops with domed foil and put into the slow cooker pot. Pour boiling water into the pot to come halfway up the sides of the mugs. Cover with the lid and cook on high for 1–1¼ hours or until the puddings are softly set in the center.

Lift the puddings out of the slow cooker pot and remove the foil. Mix the cream and mint together and pour into a pitcher. Dust the puddings with confectioners' sugar and serve immediately with the mint cream.

For gingered mousses with orange cream, add 4 teaspoons finely chopped stem ginger to the mousse mixture and cook as above. To serve, stir an extra 2 teaspoons finely chopped stem ginger and the finely grated zest of 1 orange into 6 tablespoons sour cream in a bowl.

apricot & orange fool

Preparation time **20 minutes**,
   plus cooling
Cooking temperature **low**
Cooking time **3–4 hours**
Serves **6**

1½ cups ready-to-eat dried
   apricots
grated zest and juice of
   1 **orange**
2 tablespoons **superfine sugar**
1¼ cups cold **water**
1 cup **ready-made custard**
2 cups **plain yogurt**

Preheat the slow cooker if necessary; see the manufacturer's instructions. Put the apricots, orange zest and juice, and sugar into the slow cooker pot and pour over the water. Cover with the lid and cook on low for 3–4 hours or until the apricots are plump.

Lift the pot out of the housing using oven mitts and allow the apricots to cool, then puree with an immersion blender or transfer to a blender and whiz until smooth.

Fold the custard and yogurt together until just mixed, then add the apricot puree and very lightly mix for a marbled effect. Spoon into the glasses and serve with dainty cookies.

For prune & vanilla fool, put 1½ cups ready-to-eat pitted prunes, 1 teaspoon vanilla extract, 2 tablespoons honey, and 1¼ cups cold water in the slow cooker pot and cook, cool, and make up the fool as above.

berry compote with syllabub cream

Preparation time **20 minutes**,
  plus cooling
Cooking temperature **low**
Cooking time **1¼–2 hours**
Serves **4**

3 cups **strawberries**, halved or
  quartered if large
1¾ cups **blueberries**
grated zest and juice of
  1 lemon
3 tablespoons **superfine sugar**
3 tablespoons **water**

Syllabub cream
⅔ cup **heavy cream**
2 tablespoons **superfine sugar**
grated zest of ½ **lemon**
2 tablespoons **dry white wine**
lemon zest curls or small **herb**
  or **pansy flowers**, to decorate
  (optional)

Preheat the slow cooker if necessary; see the manufacturer's instructions. Put the fruit, lemon zest and juice, sugar, and water into the slow cooker pot. Cover with the lid and cook on low for 1½–2 hours or until the fruit is tender but still holds its shape.

Lift the pot out of the housing using oven mitts and allow the compote to cool. Just before serving, make the syllabub. Pour the cream into a bowl, add the sugar and lemon zest, and whisk until it forms soft swirls. Add the white wine and whisk for 1–2 minutes more or until thick again.

Spoon the fruit into tall champagne-style glasses and top with spoonfuls of the cream. Decorate with lemon zest curls or small herb or pansy flowers, if desired, and serve immediately.

For peach compote with vanilla, halve 6 firm, ripe peaches and add to the slow cooker pot with ⅓ cup superfine sugar, ⅔ cup Marsala or sweet sherry, ⅔ cup water, and a slit vanilla bean. Cover and cook as above. Transfer the peaches to a serving dish. Scrape the seeds from the vanilla bean and add to the syrup, then discard the pod. Mix 2 teaspoons cornstarch with a little cold water to make a smooth paste, stir into the syrup in the slow cooker pot, replace the lid, and cook on high for 15 minutes. Stir well, then pour over the peaches. Sprinkle with 1 cup raspberries and allow to cool. Serve with spoonfuls of sour cream.

sticky marmalade syrup pudding

Preparation time **20 minutes**
Cooking temperature **high**
Cooking time **3–3½ hours**
Serves **4–5**

butter, for greasing
4 tablespoons **corn syrup**
3 tablespoons **orange marmalade**
1½ cups **self-rising flour**
¾ cup **vegetable suet**
¼ cup **light brown sugar**
1 teaspoon **ground ginger**
grated zest and juice of
  1 **orange**
2 **eggs**
2 tablespoons **milk**

Preheat the slow cooker if necessary; see the manufacturer's instructions. Lightly butter a 5 cup pudding mold and base-line with a circle of nonstick parchment paper, checking first that it will fit in the slow cooker pot. Spoon the corn syrup and 2 tablespoons of the marmalade into the basin.

Put the flour, suet, sugar, and ginger in a bowl and mix together. Add the remaining marmalade, orange zest and juice, the eggs, and milk and beat until smooth. Spoon the mixture into the mold, spread it level, and cover the top with buttered foil.

Lower the mold into the slow cooker pot and pour boiling water into the pot to come halfway up the sides of the mold. Cover with the lid and cook on high for 3–3½ hours or until the pudding is well risen and feels firm and dry when the top is pressed with a fingertip.

Lift the basin out of the slow cooker pot using a dish towel and remove the foil. Loosen the edge of the pudding with a knife, turn out onto a plate, and peel off the lining paper. Serve scoops of the pudding in bowls with custard or vanilla ice cream.

For sticky banana pudding, spoon 4 tablespoons corn syrup and 3 tablespoons light brown sugar into the base of the lined mold. Cut 2 bananas in half lengthwise, then in half again crosswise. Toss in the juice of ½ lemon and arrange cut side down in the bottom of the mold. Make up the pudding mixture, spoon over the bananas, and continue as above.

strawberry cheesecake

Preparation time **30 minutes**,
  plus chilling
Cooking temperature **high**
Cooking time **2–2½ hours**
Serves **4–5**

4 **sponge cakes**
1¼ cups **full-fat cream cheese**
⅛ cup **superfine sugar**
⅔ cup **heavy cream**
3 **eggs**
grated zest and juice of
  ½ lemon

Topping
2 tablespoons **strawberry jelly**
1 tablespoon **lemon juice**
1½ cups **strawberries**, hulled
  and sliced

Preheat the slow cooker if necessary; see the manufacturer's instructions. Line the base and sides of a soufflé dish, 5½ inches in diameter and 3½ inches high, with nonstick parchment paper, checking first it will fit in the slow cooker pot. Line the base with the sponge cakes, trimming them to fit in a single layer.

Put the cream cheese and sugar in a bowl, then gradually whisk in the cream until smooth and thick. Gradually whisk in the eggs one at a time, then mix in the lemon zest and juice. Pour the mixture into the dish and spread it level.

Cover the top with buttered foil and lower it into the slow cooker pot. Pour boiling water into the pot to come halfway up the sides of the dish. Cover with the lid and cook on high for 2–2½ hours or until the cheesecake is well risen and softly set in the center.

Lift the dish out of the slow cooker pot using a dish towel and leave to cool and firm up. The cheesecake will sink quickly as it cools to about the size that it was before cooking. Transfer to the refrigerator to chill for at least 4 hours.

When ready to serve, loosen the edge of the cheesecake with a knife, turn out onto a serving plate, peel off the lining paper, and turn it the right way up. Mix the jelly and lemon juice in a bowl until smooth, add the sliced strawberries, and toss together. Spoon on top of the cheesecake and serve immediately.

hot toddy oranges

Preparation time **15 minutes**
Cooking temperature **low**
Cooking time **2–3 hours**
Serves **4**

8 **clementines** or **tangerines**
2 tablespoons **honey**
⅓ cup **light brown sugar**
grated zest and juice of
   ½ **lemon**
4 tablespoons **whiskey**
1¼ cups boiling **water**
1 tablespoon **butter**

Preheat the slow cooker if necessary; see the manufacturer's instructions. Peel the clementines, leaving them whole. Put the remaining ingredients in the slow cooker pot and mix together.

Add the clementines. Cover with the lid and cook on low for 2–3 hours or until piping hot. Spoon into shallow bowls and serve with just-melting scoops of vanilla ice cream.

For hot toddy apricots, put all the ingredients, omitting the clementines and sugar, into the slow cooker pot as above. Add 2 cups ready-to-eat dried apricots and continue as above. Serve warm with sour cream or vanilla ice cream.

peppermint & raspberry brûlée

Preparation time **30 minutes**,
plus chilling
Cooking temperature **low**
Cooking time **2½–3½ hours**
Serves **4**

4 **egg yolks**
3 tablespoons **superfine sugar**
1¾ cups **heavy cream**
¼ teaspoon **peppermint extract**
1¼ cups **raspberries**
2 tablespoons **confectioners'
sugar**

Preheat the slow cooker if necessary; see the manufacturer's instructions. Whisk the egg yolks and sugar in a bowl for 3–4 minutes until frothy, then gradually whisk in the cream. Stir in the peppermint extract, then strain the egg custard into a pitcher.

Pour into 4 ramekin dishes, each ⅔ cup, checking first that they will fit in the slow cooker pot. Put the dishes into the slow cooker pot, pour boiling water into the pot to come halfway up the sides of the dishes, then loosely cover the top of each dish with foil.

Cover with the lid and cook on low for 2½–3½ hours or until the custard is set with a slight quiver to the middle. Lift the dishes carefully out of the slow cooker and allow to cool. Transfer to the refrigerator to chill for 4 hours.

When ready to serve, pile a few raspberries in the center of each dish and sprinkle over some confectioners' sugar. Caramelize the sugar with a kitchen torch.

For peppermint & white chocolate brûlée, bring 1½ cups heavy cream just to a boil in a saucepan, take off the heat, and add 4 oz good-quality white chocolate, broken into pieces, and allow to melt. Whisk the egg yolks with 2 tablespoons superfine sugar, then gradually mix in the chocolate cream and the peppermint extract. Continue as above. Replace the raspberries with blueberries and serve as above.

honeyed rice pudding

Preparation time **10 minutes**
Cooking temperature **low**
Cooking time **2½–3 hours**
Serves **4**

butter, for greasing
3 cups **whole milk**
3 tablespoons **honey**
½ cup **risotto rice**

Preheat the slow cooker if necessary; see the manufacturer's instructions. Lightly butter the inside of the slow cooker pot. Pour the milk into a saucepan, add the honey, and bring just to a boil, stirring until the honey has melted. Pour into the slow cooker pot, add the rice, and stir gently.

Cover with the lid and cook on low for 2½–3 hours, stirring once during cooking, or until the pudding is thickened and the rice is soft. Stir again just before spooning into dishes and serve topped with spoonfuls of jelly, or the Apricot Preserves on page 222, and thick cream, if desired.

For vanilla rice pudding, pour the milk into a saucepan, replace the honey with 3 tablespoons superfine sugar and bring just to a boil. Slit a vanilla bean, scrape the black seeds out with a small knife, and add to the milk with the pod. Pour into the greased slow cooker pot, add the rice, and cook as above. Remove the vanilla pod before serving with thick cream.

toffee apple pancakes

Preparation time **10 minutes**
Cooking temperature **high**
Cooking time **1–1½ hours**
Serves **4–6**

¼ cup **butter**
⅓ cup **light brown sugar**
2 tablespoons **corn syrup**
4 **dessert apples**, cored and
   each cut into 8 slices
juice of 1 **lemon**
6 **ready-made pancakes**
vanilla ice cream, to serve

Preheat the slow cooker if necessary; see the manufacturer's instructions. Heat the butter, sugar, and syrup in a saucepan or in a bowl in the microwave until the butter has just melted.

Add the apples and lemon juice to the slow cooker pot and toss together. Stir the butter mix and pour it over the apples. Cover with the lid and cook on high for 1–1½ hours or until the apples are tender but still holding their shape.

Heat the pancakes in a skillet or the microwave, according to the package instructions. Fold in half and arrange on serving plates. Stir the apple mix, then spoon it onto the pancakes. Top with a scoop of vanilla ice cream.

For toffee banana pancakes, make up the recipe as above, replacing the apples with 6 small thickly sliced bananas and adding ⅔ cup boiling water. When ready to serve, reheat 6 pancakes, spread with 3 tablespoons chocolate and hazelnut spread, then top with the bananas and ice cream.

cherry & coconut sponge pudding

Preparation time **15 minutes**
Cooking temperature **high**
Cooking time **3–3½ hours**
Serves **4–6**

butter, for greasing
½ cup **shredded coconut**
13 oz can **cherry pie filling**
1 lb package **Madeira cake mix**
4 tablespoons **sunflower oil** or 1 **egg** (see cake mix instructions)

Preheat the slow cooker if necessary; see the manufacturer's instructions. Lightly butter a 6 cup pudding mold and base-line with a circle of nonstick parchment paper, checking first it will fit in the slow cooker pot. Sprinkle in a little of the coconut, then tilt and turn the basin until the buttery sides are lightly coated. Spoon half the cherry pie filling into the base of the basin.

Tip the cake mix into a bowl and mix in the oil or egg and water according to the package instructions. Stir in the remaining coconut, then spoon the mixture into the mold and spread it level. Cover the top with buttered, domed foil and lower the basin into the slow cooker pot.

Pour boiling water into the slow cooker pot to come halfway up the sides of the mold. Cover with the lid and cook on high for 3–3½ hours or until the pudding is well risen, feels dry, and springs back when pressed with a fingertip.

Lift the mold out of the slow cooker pot using a dish towel and remove the foil. Loosen the edge of the pudding with a knife, turn out onto a plate, and peel off the lining paper. Heat the remaining pie filling in a small saucepan or the microwave until hot. Serve the pudding in bowls with the warm cherries and scoops of vanilla ice cream, if desired.

For spiced chocolate cherry sponge pudding, line the pudding mold with cherry pie filling as above, omitting the coconut. Make up a 1 lb chocolate-flavored Madeira cake mix with 1 teaspoon ground cinnamon and the sunflower oil or egg and continue as above.

raspberry & rhubarb oaty crumble

Preparation time **15 minutes**
Cooking temperature **low**
Cooking time **2–3 hours**
Serves **4**

13 oz trimmed **rhubarb**
1¼ cups frozen **raspberries**
¼ cup **superfine sugar**
3 tablespoons **water**

Topping
1 tablespoon **butter**
3 tablespoons **slivered
  almonds**
4 **granola bars**

Preheat the slow cooker if necessary; see the manufacturer's instructions. Cut the rhubarb into 1 inch thick slices and add to the slow cooker pot with the still-frozen raspberries, the sugar, and water. Cover with the lid and cook on low for 2–3 hours or until the rhubarb is just tender.

When almost ready to serve, heat the butter in a skillet, add the almonds and crumble in the granola bars. Fry, stirring, for 3–4 minutes or until hot and lightly browned. Spoon the fruit into bowls, sprinkle the crumble over the top, and serve with thick cream.

For peach & mixed berry crumble, dice 3 fresh peaches, discarding the pits, and add to the slow cooker pot with 1¼ cups mixed still-frozen summer fruits, the sugar, and water. Cook and sprinkle with the granola crumble topping as above.

chocolate croissant pudding

Preparation time **15 minutes**
Cooking temperature **low**
Cooking time **4–4½ hours**
Serves **4**

¼ cup **butter**
4 **chocolate croissants**
¼ cup **superfine sugar**
¼ teaspoon **ground cinnamon**
⅓ cup **pecan nuts**, roughly
   crushed
1¼ cups **milk**
2 **eggs**
2 **egg yolks**
1 teaspoon **vanilla extract**

Butter the inside of a 5 cup straight-sided heatproof dish with a little of the butter, checking first that it will fit into the slow cooker pot.

Slice the croissants thickly and spread one side of each slice with the remaining butter. Mix together the sugar and spice. Arrange the croissants in layers in the dish, sprinkling each layer with the spiced sugar and the pecans.

Whisk the milk, whole eggs, egg yolks, and vanilla extract in a bowl. Pour into the dish and allow to soak for 15 minutes. Preheat the slow cooker if necessary; see the manufacturer's instructions.

Cover the top of the dish loosely with buttered foil and lower it into the slow cooker pot. Pour boiling water into the pot to come halfway up the sides of the dish, cover with the lid, and cook on low for 4–4½ hours or until the custard is set and the pudding well risen. Lift the dish out of the slow cooker pot using a dish towel. Dust with sifted confectioners' sugar. Scoop into bowls and serve with cream.

For bread & butter pudding, spread 3 tablespoons butter over 4 thick slices of bread, cut into triangles, and layer in the buttered dish with 3 tablespoons luxury mixed dried fruit and the sugar. Pour the custard over the bread and continue as above.

drinks &
preserves

beet chutney

Preparation time **30 minutes**
Cooking temperature **high**
Cooking time **6–7 hours**
Makes **4** jars of assorted sizes

1 bunch of raw **beets**, about 5
  in total, trimmed and peeled
1 lb **red plums**, pitted and
  roughly chopped
1 large **onion**, finely chopped
1 cup **red wine vinegar**
1 cup **light brown sugar**
1½ inches **fresh ginger root**,
  peeled and finely chopped
1 tablespoon **star anise**
  pieces, crushed
1 teaspoon **peppercorns**,
  crushed
1 teaspoon **ground cinnamon**

Preheat the slow cooker if necessary; see the manufacturer's instructions. Coarsely grate the beets and put them into the slow cooker pot with all the remaining ingredients.

Mix everything together thoroughly, then cover with the lid and cook on high for 6–7 hours, stirring once or twice, until the beets are tender and the plums pulpy.

Warm 4 clean jars in a low oven for 5 minutes. Ladle the hot chutney into the warm jars, cover the surface with waxed disks, and screw the lids in place. Label and store in a cool place until required. Once opened, store in the refrigerator.

Serve with cheese, cold sliced ham, or with the Zucchini & Fava Bean Frittata (see pages 66–67).

For chilied beet & tomato chutney, make up the chutney as the recipe above, replacing the plums with 1 lb diced tomatoes and the ginger and spices with 1 teaspoon smoked paprika, 1 teaspoon crushed dried red pepper flakes, 1 teaspoon ground cinnamon, ½ teaspoon ground allspice, and salt and pepper.

apple, thyme, & rosemary jelly

Preparation time **40 minutes**
Cooking temperature **high**
Cooking time **2–3 hours**
Makes **3** jars of assorted sizes

2 lb **cooking apples** (not
    peeled or cored), washed
    and diced
½ cup **red wine** or **cider
    vinegar**
2½ cups boiling **water**
about 2½ cups **granulated
    sugar**
1 tablespoon **thyme leaves**,
    stripped from the stems
2 tablespoons finely chopped
    rosemary leaves

Preheat the slow cooker if necessary; see the manufacturer's instructions. Put the apples and vinegar into the slow cooker pot and pour over the boiling water. Cover with the lid and cook on high for 2–3 hours or until the apples are tender. Don't worry if the apples discolor.

Hang a jelly bag from a frame or upturned stool and set a bowl beneath it. Ladle the cooked apples and their juices into the bag and allow to drip through.

Measure the liquid and pour it into a large saucepan; for every 2½ cups liquid add 2 cups of sugar. Heat gently, stirring occasionally, until the sugar has dissolved, then boil rapidly for about 15 minutes until setting point is reached. Check with a candy thermometer or spoon a little of the jelly onto a saucer that has been chilled in the refrigerator. Leave for 1–2 minutes, then run a finger through the jelly. If a finger space is left and the jelly has wrinkled it is ready; if not boil for 5–10 minutes more and then retest.

Skim any scum with a slotted spoon, then stir in the chopped herbs. Allow the jelly to stand for 5 minutes.

Warm 3 clean jars in a low oven for 5 minutes. Ladle the jelly into the warm jars, cover the surface with waxed disks, add transparent jam pot covers, and secure with elastic bands. Label and store in a cool place. Once opened, store in the refrigerator. Serve with lamb.

For apple & blackberry jelly, put 1½ lb cooking apples, washed and diced, into the slow cooker pot with 2 cups blackberries, ½ cup lemon juice, and the boiling water. Continue as above, omitting the herbs. Serve with scones.

orange marmalade

Preparation time **45 minutes,**
plus overnight cooling
Cooking temperature **low**
Cooking time **8–10 hours**
Makes **6** jars of assorted sizes

2 lb **Seville oranges**
5 cups boiling **water**
8 cups **preserving** or
  granulated sugar

Preheat the slow cooker if necessary; see the manufacturer's instructions. Put the whole oranges into the slow cooker pot, cover with the boiling water, and put an upturned saucer on top of the oranges to stop them from floating.

Cover with the lid and cook on low for 8–10 hours or until the oranges are tender. Lift the pot out of the housing using oven mitts and allow to cool overnight. The next day, lift the oranges out of the slow cooker pot, draining well. Cut into quarters, scoop out and discard the seeds, then thinly slice the oranges.

Put the sliced oranges and the liquid from the slow cooker pot into a preserving pan or large saucepan, add the sugar, and heat gently, stirring occasionally until the sugar has completely dissolved. Increase the heat, and boil for 20–30 minutes or until setting point is reached (see page 216).

Warm 6 clean jars in a low oven for 5 minutes. Ladle the hot marmalade into the warm jars, cover the surface with waxed disks, add transparent jam pot covers, and secure with elastic bands or screw the jar lids in place. Label and store in a cool place until required.

For dark ginger orange marmalade, cook the Seville oranges with ¾ cup peeled and finely chopped fresh ginger root in the slow cooker as above. Make up the marmalade with the sliced oranges and ginger as above, using 7 cups preserving or granulated sugar and 2 cups light brown sugar.

passion fruit & lime curd

Preparation time **15 minutes**
Cooking temperature **low**
Cooking time **3–4 hours**
Makes **3** small jars

½ cup **unsalted butter**, diced
1¾ cups **superfine sugar**
4 **eggs**, beaten
grated zest and juice of
   2 **limes**
grated zest of 2 **lemons**
juice of 1 **lemon**
3 **passion fruit**, halved

Preheat the slow cooker if necessary; see the manufacturer's instructions. Put the butter and sugar in a large bowl, checking first that it will fit into the slow cooker pot, then heat in the microwave until the butter has just melted. Alternatively, heat the butter and sugar in a saucepan and pour into the bowl.

Stir the sugar mix, then gradually whisk in the eggs, and then the fruit zest and juice. Cover the bowl with foil and lower into the slow cooker pot. Pour boiling water into the pot to come halfway up the sides of the bowl. Cover with the lid and cook on low for 3–4 hours, stirring once during cooking, until thick.

Stir once more, then scoop the passion fruit seeds out of the halved fruit with a teaspoon and stir them into the curd.

Warm 3 clean jars in a low oven for 5 minutes. Ladle the curd into the warm jars, cover the surface with waxed disks, add transparent jam pot covers, and secure with elastic bands or screw the lids in place. Label and allow to cool. The curd can be stored for up to 2 weeks in the refrigerator.

For lemon curd, make up as above, using the zest and juice of 3 lemons and omitting the lime zest and juice and passion fruit.

apricot preserves

Preparation time **15 minutes**
Cooking temperature **high**
Cooking time **3–5 hours**
Makes **3** jars of assorted sizes

2 cups ready-to-eat dried
apricots, diced
4 **peaches**, halved, pitted,
and diced
1 cup **superfine sugar**
1¼ cups boiling **water**

Preheat the slow cooker if necessary; see the manufacturer's instructions. Put the apricots, peaches, sugar, and boiling water into the slow cooker pot and stir together.

Cover with the lid and cook on high for 3–5 hours, stirring once during cooking and then again at the end, until the fruit is soft and the liquid thick and syrupy, with a texture like chutney.

Warm 3 clean jars in a low oven for 5 minutes. Ladle the preserve into the warm jars. Cover the surface with waxed disks, add transparent jam pot covers, and secure with elastic bands or screw the jar lids in place. Label and allow to cool. The preserve can be stored for up to 2 months in the refrigerator.

For apricot & orange preserves, put 2⅔ cups dried apricots, the grated zest and juice of 1 large orange, the sugar, and the boiling water in the slow cooker pot, omitting the peaches. Continue as above.

hot spiced berry punch

Preparation time **10 minutes**
Cooking temperature **high and low**
Cooking time **3–4 hours**
Serves **6**

4 cups **cranberry and raspberry drink**
2 cups frozen **berry fruits**
¼ cup **superfine sugar**
4 tablespoons **crème de cassis** (optional)
4 small **star anise**
1 **cinnamon stick**, halved lengthwise
fresh **raspberries**, to decorate (optional)

Preheat the slow cooker if necessary; see the manufacturer's instructions. Pour the cranberry and raspberry drink into the slow cooker pot. Add the frozen fruits, the sugar, and crème de cassis, if using. Stir together, then add the star anise and halved cinnamon stick.

Cover with the lid and cook on high for 1 hour. Reduce the heat and cook on low for 2–3 hours, or set to auto for 3–4 hours, until piping hot.

Strain, if desired, then put the star anise and cinnamon into small heatproof glasses. Ladle the hot punch into the glasses and add a few fresh raspberries, if desired.

For boozy berry punch, replace the crème de cassis with ⅔ cup vodka and make up the recipe as above.

For spiced berry and pear compote, make up the punch as above. Peel, core, and slice 4 ripe pears and arrange in a heatproof serving dish. Pour over 1¼ cups of the hot punch and allow to cool. Serve as a dessert or breakfast accompaniment topped with spoonfuls of whole milk yogurt flavored with a little honey. Serve the remaining hot punch in glasses as above.

cider toddy

Preparation time **10 minutes**

Cooking temperature **high** and
   low

Cooking time **3–4 hours**

Serves **6**

1 litre 4 cups **hard cider**

½ cup **whiskey**

½ cup **orange juice**

4 tablespoons **honey**

2 **cinnamon sticks**

orange wedges and **curls**, to
   decorate (optional)

Preheat the slow cooker if necessary; see the manufacturer's instructions. Add all the ingredients to the slow cooker pot, cover with the lid, and cook on high for 1 hour.

Reduce the heat and cook on low for 2–3 hours, or set to auto for 3–4 hours, until piping hot. Stir, then ladle into heatproof tumblers. Add orange wedges and curls to decorate, if desired.

For gingered cider toddy, replace the whiskey with ½ cup ginger wine and 2 tablespoons finely chopped stem ginger and make up the recipe as above.

For citrus toddy, pour ⅔ cup whiskey into the slow cooker pot, add 4 tablespoons honey, ½ cup superfine sugar, and 3 cups cold water, then add the grated zest of 1 orange, the juice of 3 oranges, the grated zest of 1 lemon, and the juice of 3 lemons. Roughly crush 8 cardamom pods, add the pods and seeds to the slow cooker pot. Cover and cook as above.

mulled wine

Preparation time **5 minutes**
Cooking temperature **high** and
   low
Cooking time **3–4 hours**
Serves **6**

3 cups or 1 bottle inexpensive
   red wine
1¼ cups **clear apple juice**
1¼ cups **water**
juice of 1 **orange**
1 **orange**, sliced
½ **lemon**, sliced
1 **cinnamon stick**, halved
6 **cloves**
2 **bay leaves**
½ cup **superfine sugar**
⅔ cup **brandy**

Preheat the slow cooker if necessary; see the manufacturer's instructions. Pour the wine, apple juice, water, and orange juice into the slow cooker pot.

Add the sliced orange and lemon, the cinnamon stick, cloves, and bay leaves, then mix in the sugar and brandy.

Cover with the lid and cook on high for 1 hour. Reduce the heat and cook on low for 2–3 hours, or set to auto for 3–4 hours, until piping hot. Ladle into heatproof glasses.

For cranberry mulled wine, replace the apple juice with 1¼ cups cranberry juice and 1 cup fresh cranberries and make up the recipe as above.

For mulled wine dessert, cook the mulled wine as above. Spoon 6 tablespoons cold water into a bowl, sprinkle over 4 tablespoons gelatin, allow to soak for 5 minutes. Strain the mulled wine, stir in the gelatin until dissolved, then cool. Pour into 8 wine glasses and chill in the refrigerator until set. Top each of the mulled wine desserts with whipped cream.

hot buttered rum

Preparation time **5 minutes**
Cooking temperature **high** and
   low
Cooking time **3–4 hours**
Serves **6**

4 cups **clear apple juice**
⅔ cups **dark rum**
2 tablespoons **honey**
2 tablespoons **dark brown**
   sugar
2 tablespoons **butter**
6 **cloves**
1 **dessert apple**, cored and
   thickly sliced, to decorate

Preheat the slow cooker if necessary; see the manufacturer's instructions. Put the apple juice, rum, honey, sugar, butter, and cloves into the slow cooker pot.

Cover with the lid and cook on high for 1 hour. Reduce the heat and cook on low for 2–3 hours, or set to auto for 3–4 hours, until piping hot.

Stir, scoop out the cloves, then ladle the punch into heatproof tumblers. Decorate with slices of apple.

For hot buttered calvados, replace the rum with ⅔ cup calvados (apple brandy) and make up the recipe as above.

For poached apples with buttered rum, once the punch is made pour into a serving pitcher keeping 1¼ cups in the slow cooker pot. Add 4 medium-sized cooking apples that have been quartered, cored, and peeled, cover, and cook on high for 1–1½ hours until the apples are tender. Serve as a dessert with scoops of vanilla ice cream.

skier's hot chocolate

Preparation time **10 minutes**
Cooking temperature **low**
Cooking time **2–3 hours**
Serves **4**

4 oz good-quality **chocolate**
2 tablespoons **superfine
  sugar**
3 cups **whole milk**
few drops of **vanilla extract**
little **ground cinnamon**
3 tablespoons **Kahlúa coffee
  liqueur** (optional)
mini marshmallows, to serve

Preheat the slow cooker if necessary; see the manufacturer's instructions. Put the chocolate and sugar in the slow cooker pot, then add the milk, vanilla extract, and cinnamon.

Cover with the lid and cook on low for 2–3 hours, whisking once or twice, until the chocolate has melted and the drink is hot. Stir in the Kahlúa, if using. Ladle into mugs and top with a few mini marshmallows.

For hot chocolate with brandy cream, make up the hot chocolate as above, replacing the Kahlua with 3 tablespoons brandy. Whip ½ cup heavy cream with 2 tablespoons of confectioners' sugar until soft peaks form, then gradually whisk in 3 tablespoons brandy. Pour the hot chocolate into mugs, then top with spoonfuls of the whipped cream and dust lightly with drinking chocolate powder or grated chocolate.

For Mexican hot chocolate, put ½ cup unsweetened cocoa powder and 4 teaspoons instant coffee into the slow cooker pot. Measure 4 cups of boiling water. Make a smooth paste by mixing a little of the boiling water with the cocoa and coffee. Add the rest of the water, ⅔ cup rum, ½ cup superfine sugar, ½ teaspoon ground cinnamon, and 1 dried red chili, cut in half. Cover and cook on low for 3–4 hours. Discard the chili and ladle into 4 cups. Top with ⅔ cup heavy cream.

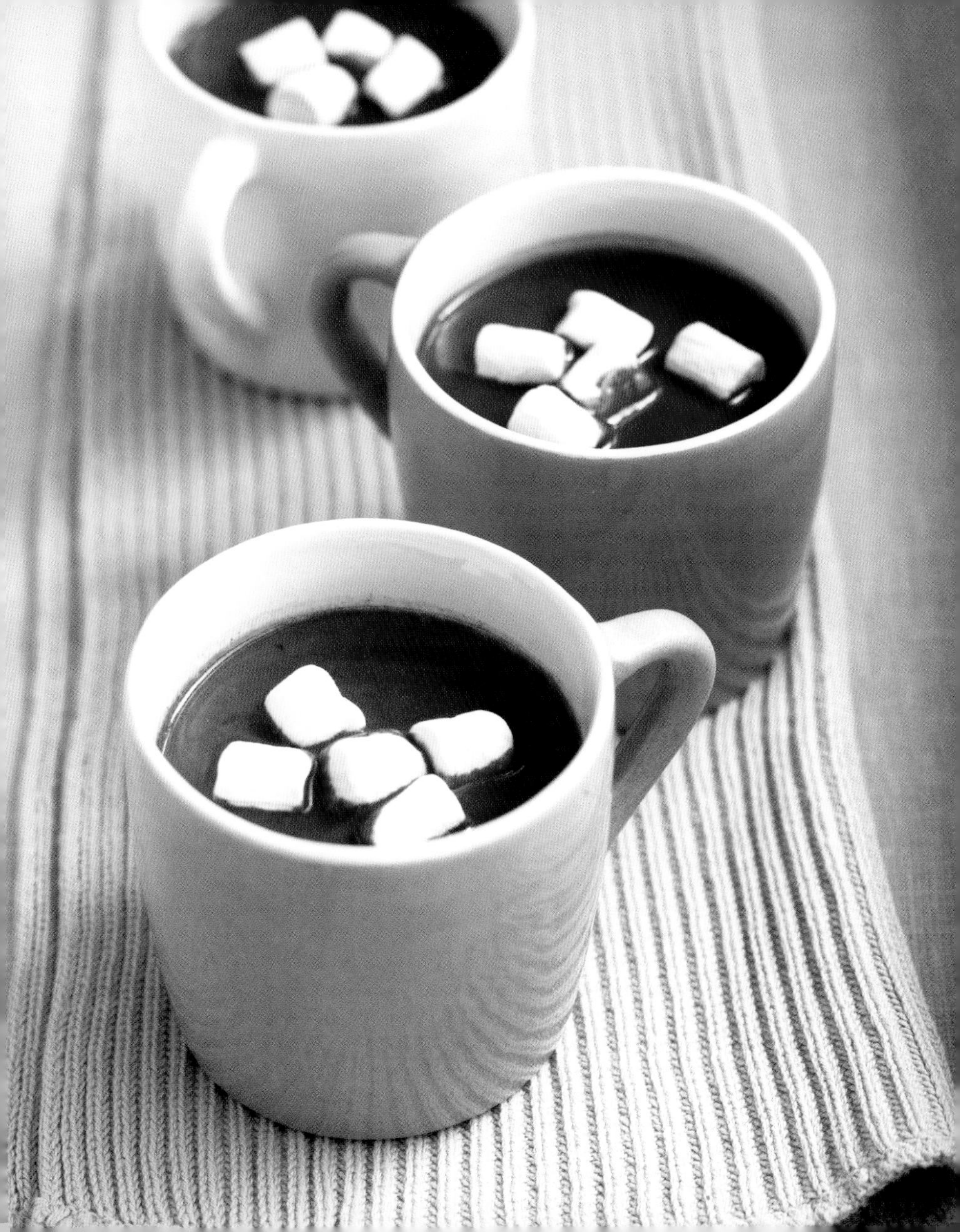

index

almonds
chicken & almond pilaf
134
cider poached apples
with granola 180
creamy chicken korma
154
raspberry & rhubarb oaty
crumble 208
topsy turvy plum pudding
186
apple juice
hot buttered rum 230
mulled wine 228
apples
apple & blackberry jelly
216
apple, thyme, & rosemary
jelly 216
baked mackerel with
beets 78
balsamic braised pork
chops 94
cider poached apples
with granola 180
duck, pork, & apple
rillettes 62
mulligatawny soup 20
poached apples with
spiced poached apples
with orange 180
toffee apple pancakes
204
apricots
apricot & orange fool
199
apricot & orange
preserves 222
apricot & pistachio
stuffed pork tenderloin
168
apricot preserves 222
eggplant timbale 140
hot toddy apricots 198
Asian glazed ribs 114

asparagus
salmon & asparagus
risotto 174
Thai broth with fish
dumplings 46
zucchini, salmon, &
asparagus frittata 66
avgolemono
chicken avgolemono
118
salmon avgolemono 118
avocado & red onion salsa
158

bacon
cheesy bacon & rosemary
tortilla 54
chicken & sage hotpot 76
eggs Benedict 56
garlicky pork & sage pâté
52
haddock & bacon
chowder 26
leek, potato, & Stilton
soup 38
minestrone soup 36
New Orleans chicken
gumbo 162
prune stuffed pork
tenderloin 168
slow-cooked lamb shanks
with prunes 172
turkey & cranberry
meatloaf 64
turkey & sausage stew
80
vegetable broth with
dumplings 18
balsamic vinegar
balsamic braised pork
chops 94
balsamic tomatoes with
spaghetti 142
baltis
cauliflower & spinach
balti 138
chicken & sweet potato
balti 92
mushroom & sweet
potato balti 138

bananas
mini banana & date
puddings 178
mini chocolate & banana
puddings 178
sticky banana pudding
194
toffee banana pancakes
204
beans
baked salmon with basil
bean mash 112
chicken & navy bean
stew 86
chilied beef with
chocolate 158
chilied stuffed peppers
144
hot Spanish beans 106
mustard beans 106
pepperonata & white
bean stew 132
smoked cod with bean
mash 112
traditional cottage pie 82
beef
beef & Guinness puff pie
170
chilied beef with
chocolate 158
Indian spiced cottage pie
82
keema mutter 102
mustardy beef hotpot 76
stifado 116
tamarind beef with ginger
beer 164
traditional cottage pie 82
beets
baked mackerel with
beets 78
beet & mascarpone
risotto 126
beet chutney 214
chilied beet & tomato
chutney 214
venison puff pie 152
bell peppers
baked seafood with
saffron 96

chicken & navy bean
stew 86
chilied corn 68
chilied stuffed peppers
144
eggplant ratatouille with
baked eggs 130
herby stuffed peppers
144
New Orleans chicken
gumbo 162
pepperonata 132
red pepper & chorizo
tortilla 54
roasted vegetable terrine
70
sweet & sour pork 108
tomato & red pepper
soup 30
tomato-braised squid
with chorizo 104
vegetable goulash 124
warm lentil & feta salad
60
berry fruits
hot spiced berry punch
224
spiced berry and pear
compote 224
black bean sauce: pork
with black bean
sauce 108
blackberries
apple & blackberry jelly
216
topsy turvy plum pudding
186
blue cheese: barley risotto
with blue cheese 136
blueberries
berry compote with
syllabub cream 192
peppermint & white
chocolate brûlée 200
brandy: mulled wine 228
butternut squash
butternut & orange
soup 28
Thai coconut & butternut
soup 28

calvados: hot buttered calvados 230

cannellini beans
  baked salmon with basil bean mash 112
  smoked cod with bean mash 112

carrots
  baked mackerel with beet 78
  beery beef hotpot 170
  carrot & cumin soup 34
  chicken & sage hotpot 75
  chicken & tortelloni soup 24
  fragrant spiced chicken with chili 110
  gingered carrot soup 20
  honey-glazed ham 100
  Indian spiced cottage pie 82
  Irish stew 72
  lamb & barley broth 32
  minestrone soup 36
  mulligatawny soup 20
  old English pea & ham soup 22
  turkey & sausage stew 80
  vegetable broth with dumplings 18
  vegetable goulash 124

cauliflower
  cauliflower & spinach balti 138
  cheesy cauliflower soup 48

cheese
  barley risotto with blue cheese 136
  beef & Guinness puff pie 170
  beet & mascarpone risotto 126
  caramelized onion soup 432
  cheesy bacon & rosemary tortilla 54

cheesy cauliflower soup 48
creamy paneer korma 154
French onion soup 42
leek, potato, & Stilton soup 38
strawberry cheesecake 196
warm lentil & feta salad 60

cheesecake: strawberry cheesecake 196

cherry
  cherry & coconut sponge pudding 206
  spiced chocolate cherry sponge pudding 206

chicken
  chicken & almond pilaf 134
  chicken & chorizo tagliatelle 84
  chicken & navy bean stew 86
  chicken & sage hotpot 76
  chicken & sweet potato balti 92
  chicken & tortelloni soup 24
  chicken avgolemono 118
  chicken broth with mini herb dumplings 18
  chicken, pork, & prune rillettes 62
  cock-a-leekie soup 38
  creamy chicken korma 154
  fragrant spiced chicken with chili 110
  harissa baked chicken with sweet potato 92
  Italian spiced chicken with pesto 110
  New Orleans chicken gumbo 162
  Spanish chicken with chorizo 86

chicken livers: garlicky pork & sage paté 52

chilies
  chilied beef with chocolate 158
  chilied beet & tomato chutney 214
  fragrant spiced chicken with chili 110

chocolate
  chilied beef with chocolate 158
  chocolate & coffee custard creams 184
  hot chocolate mousses 188
  Mexican hot chocolate 232
  mini banana & date puddings 178
  mini chocolate & banana puddings 178
  peppermint & white chocolate brûlée 200
  skier's hot chocolate 232

chocolate croissant pudding 210

chorizo
  chicken & chorizo tagliatelle 84
  hot Spanish beans 106
  New Orleans chicken gumbo 162
  red pepper & chorizo tortilla 54
  Spanish chicken with chorizo 86
  tomato-braised squid with chorizo 104
  tomato, lentil, & chorizo soup 44

chutneys
  beet chutney 214
  chilied beet & tomato chutney 214

cider
  apricot & pistachio stuffed pork tenderloin 168
  cider poached apples with granola 180

cider toddy 226
cider-braised pork 94
  duck, pork, & apple rillettes 62
gingered cider toddy 226
citrus toddy 226
cock-a-leekie soup 38
coconut: cherry & coconut sponge pudding 206
coconut cream: Thai coconut & butternut soup 28

cod
  fish terrine 58
  salmon-wrapped cod with leeks 150
  smoked cod with bean mash 112
  smoked cod with buttered leeks 150
  Thai broth with fish dumplings 46

coffee: chocolate & coffee custard creams 184

corn
  chicken & navy bean stew 86
  chilied corn 68
  haddock & bacon chowder 26

cottage pies
  Indian spiced cottage pie 82
  traditional 82

couscous: lemon couscous 74

crab
  crab gumbo 40
  crab gumbo soup 162
  salmon & crab chowder 26

cranberries
  braised duck with cranberries & port 156
  cranberry mulled wine 228
  turkey & cranberry meatloaf 64
  turkey & cranberry puff pie 80

turkey & sausage stew 80

crumbles
peach & mixed berry crumble 208
raspberry & rhubarb oaty crumble 208

cucumbers
baked mackerel with hot potato salad 78
pickled cucumber 114

curry: tomato & squash curry 128

custard: apricot & orange fool 190

dates
eggplant timbale 140
mini banana & date puddings 178
spiced date & chickpea pilaf 134

dhal
spinach & egg tarka dhal 146
tarka dhal 146

drinks
boozy berry punch 224
cider toddy 226
citrus toddy 228
cranberry mulled wine 228
gingered cider toddy 226
hot buttered calvados 232
hot buttered rum 230
hot spiced berry punch 224
Mexican hot chocolate 232
mulled wine 228

duck
braised duck with cranberries & port 156
braised duck with orange sauce 156
duck, pork, & apple rillettes 62

dumplings
chicken broth with mini herb dumplings 18
lamb stew with dumplings 72
Thai broth with fish dumplings 46
turkey & sausage stew 80
vegetable broth with dumplings 18

eggplants
baked eggs on toast 56
cheesy bacon & rosemary tortilla 54
chicken avgolemono 118
chocolate & coffee custard creams 184
chocolate croissant pudding 210
eggplant ratatouille with baked eggs 130
eggplant timbale 140
eggplants with baked eggs 130
tomato, lentil, & eggplant soup 44

eggs
eggs Benedict 56
hot chocolate mousses 188
peppermint & raspberry brûlée 200
red pepper & chorizo tortilla 54
smoked fish kedgeree 174
spinach & egg tarka dhal 146

fava beans:
zucchini & fava bean frittata 66

feta cheese
warm lentil & feta salad 60

fish
baked mackerel with beet 78

baked mackerel with hot potato salad 78
baked salmon with basil bean mash 112
baked salmon with pesto 96
fish pie 166
fish terrine 58
haddock & bacon chowder 26
lentil salad with sardines & peas 60
mixed fish & spinach gratin 166
salmon & asparagus risotto 174
salmon & crab chowder 26
salmon avgolemono 118
salmon steaks with lemon & tarragon foam 160
salmon-wrapped cod with leeks 150
smoked cod with bean mash 112
smoked cod with buttered leeks 150
smoked fish kedgeree 174
smoked haddock & chive terrine 58
Thai broth with fish dumplings 46
trout spirals with lemon foam 160

fools
apricot & orange fool 190
prune & vanilla fool 190

frittata
zucchini & fava bean frittata 66
zucchini, salmon, & asparagus frittata 66

ginger
dark ginger orange marmalade 218
ginger & cilantro croutes 164

gingered carrot soup 20
gingered cider toddy 226
gingered mousses with orange cream 188
ginger beer: tamarind beef with ginger beer 164
ginger wine: gingered cider toddy 226
gnocchi: pepperonata 132
goulash
pork goulash 124
vegetable goulash 124
granola: cider poached apples with granola 180
green lentils
cauliflower & spinach balti 138
Moroccan meatballs 74
Guinness: beef & Guinness puff pie 170
gumbos
crab gumbo 40
crab gumbo soup 162
mixed vegetable gumbo 40
New Orleans chicken gumbo 162

haddock
fish pie 166
fish terrine 58
haddock & bacon chowder 26
mixed fish & spinach gratin 166
smoked fish kedgeree 174
smoked haddock & chive terrine 58
ham
glazed ham with pease pudding 100
ham & leek suet pudding 88
honey-glazed ham 100
old English pea & ham soup 22
harissa baked chicken with sweet potato 92

honey
Asian glazed ribs 114
cider toddy 226
honey-glazed ham 100
honeyed rice pudding 202
hot buttered rum 230
hot toddy oranges 198
prune & vanilla fool 190
slow-cooked lamb shanks 172
hotpots
beery beef hotpot 170
chicken & sage hotpot 76
mustardy beef hotpot 76
Hungarian chorba 32

Irish stew 72
Italian spiced chicken with pesto 110

jelly: jelly roly-poly pudding 182
jellies
apple & blackberry jelly 216
apple, thyme, & rosemary jelly 216

kedgeree: smoked fish kedgeree 174
keema aloo 102
keema mutter 102

lamb
Hungarian chorba 32
Irish stew 72
keema aloo 102
lamb & barley broth 32
lamb & mushroom puff pie 152
lamb stew with dumplings 72
lamb stifado 116
pot roast lamb with rosemary 98
slow-cooked lamb shanks 172
slow-cooked lamb shanks with prunes 172

leeks
fish pie 166
ham & leek suet pudding 88
lamb & barley broth 32
leek, potato, & Stilton soup 38
salmon-wrapped cod with leeks 150
smoked cod with buttered leeks 150
turkey & sausage stew 80
vegetable broth with dumplings 18
lemons
lemon couscous 74
lemon curd 220
passion fruit & lime curd 220
pesto & lemon soup 24
salmon steaks with lemon & tarragon foam 160
trout spirals with lemon foam 160
lentils see green lentils; puy lentils; red lentils
limes : passion fruit & lime curd 220

macaroni
chicken avgolemono 118
mushroom pastichio 122
mackerel
baked mackerel with beet 78
baked mackerel with hot potato salad 78
marmalade
dark ginger orange marmalade 218
orange marmalade 218
sticky marmalade syrup pudding 194
mascarpone cheese: beet & mascarpone risotto 126
Mexican hot chocolate 232
minestrone soup 36
Moroccan meatballs 74

mousses
gingered mousses with orange cream 188
hot chocolate mousses 188
mulled wine 228
mulled wine dessert 228
mulligatawny soup 20
mushrooms
barley risotto with garlic & cilantro cream 136
beef & Guinness puff pie 170
chilied mushrooms 68
lamb & mushroom puff pie 152
mushroom & sweet potato balti 138
mushroom & thyme risotto 126
mushroom & tomato rigatoni 122
mushroom pastichio 122
sausage tagliatelle 84
sweet & sour pork 108
tomato-braised squid with chorizo 104
vegetable goulash 124
mussels: baked seafood with saffron 96
mustard
baked mackerel with beet 78
honey-glazed ham 100
mustard beans 106
mustardy beef hotpot 76

navy beans
chicken & navy bean stew 86
hot Spanish beans 106
pepperonata & white bean stew 132
New Orleans chicken gumbo 162
noodles
fragrant spiced chicken with chili 110
Thai broth with noodles & shrimp 46

okra
crab gumbo 40
New Orleans chicken gumbo 162
onions
avocado & red onion salsa 158
caramelized onion soup 42
French onion soup 42
spiced date & chickpea pilaf 134
tomato-braised squid with red onion 104
orange juice: cider toddy 226
oranges
apricot & orange fool 190
apricot & orange preserves 222
braised duck with orange sauce 156
butternut & orange soup 28
dark ginger orange marmalade 218
gingered mousses with orange cream 188
hot toddy oranges 198
mulled wine 228
orange marmalade 218
spiced poached apples with orange 180
spotted dick 182

pancakes
toffee apple pancakes 204
toffee banana pancakes 204
paneer: creamy paneer korma 154
Parmesan cheese
cheesy bacon & rosemary tortilla 54
cheesy cauliflower soup 48
parsnips
Irish stew 72

lamb & barley broth 32
spiced parsnip soup 34
split pea & parsnip soup 22
vegetable broth with dumplings 18
passion fruit & lime curd 220
pastichio: mushroom pastichio 122
pâté: garlicky pork & sage pâté 52
peaches
apricot preserves 222
peach & chocolate pudding 186
peach & mixed berry crumble 208
peach compote with vanilla 192
pearl barley
barley risotto with blue cheese 136
barley risotto with garlic & cilantro cream 136
lamb & barley broth 32
vegetable broth with dumplings 18
peppermint
peppermint & raspberry brûlée 200
peppermint & white chocolate brûlée 200
pepperonata 132
pepperonata & white bean stew 132
pesto
baked salmon with pesto 96
Italian spiced chicken with pesto 110
minestrone soup 36
pesto & lemon soup 24
pesto baked tomatoes 142
scallion & basil pesto 30
pies
beef & Guinness puff pie 170

fish pie 166
Indian spiced cottage pie 82
lamb & mushroom puff pie 152
traditional cottage pie 82
turkey & cranberry puff pie 80
venison puff pie 152
pilafs
chicken & almond pilaf 134
spiced date & chickpea pilaf 134
pistachio nuts
apricot & pistachio stuffed pork tenderloin 168
eggplant timbale 140
plums
beet chutney 214
topsy turvy plum pudding 186
pork
apricot & pistachio stuffed pork tenderloin 168
Asian glazed ribs 114
balsamic braised pork chops 94
chicken, pork, & prune rillettes 62
cider-braised pork 94
duck, pork, & apple rillettes 62
garlicky pork & sage pâté 52
pork goulash 124
pork with black bean sauce 108
prune stuffed pork tenderloin 168
sweet & sour pork 108
port: braised duck with cranberries & port 156
potatoes
baked mackerel with hot potato salad 78
beery beef hotpot 170

cheesy cauliflower soup 48
chicken & navy bean stew 86
chicken & sage hotpot 76
crushed new potatoes with rosemary cream 98
fish pie 166
haddock & bacon chowder 26
honey-glazed ham 100
Indian spiced cottage pie 82
Irish stew 72
keema aloo 102
leek, potato, & Stilton soup 38
red pepper & chorizo tortilla 54
slow-cooked lamb shanks 172
traditional cottage pie 82
vegetable goulash 124
preserved lemons: slow-cooked lamb shanks 172
preserves
apple & blackberry jelly 216
apple, thyme, & rosemary jelly 216
apricot & orange preserves 222
apricot preserves 222
beet chutney 214
chilied beet & tomato chutney 214
dark ginger orange marmalade 218
lemon curd 220
orange marmalade 218
passion fruit & lime curd 220
prunes
chicken, pork, & prune rillettes 62
cock-a-leekie soup 38

prune & vanilla fool 190
prune stuffed pork tenderloin 168
slow-cooked lamb shanks with prunes 172
punches
boozy berry punch 224
hot spiced berry punch 224
puy lentils
lentil salad with sardines & peas 60
warm lentil & feta salad 60

quinoa: eggplants with baked eggs 130

raspberries
hot spiced berry punch 224
peach compote with vanilla 192
peppermint & raspberry brûlée 200
raspberry & rhubarb oaty crumble 208
ratatouille: eggplant ratatouille with baked eggs 130
red kidney beans
chilied beef with chocolate 158
chilied stuffed peppers 144
red lentils
Indian spiced cottage pie 82
mulligatawny soup 20
tarka dhal 146
tomato, lentil, & eggplant soup 44
tomato, lentil, & chorizo soup 44
rhubarb: raspberry & rhubarb oaty crumble 208

rice
beet & mascarpone risotto 126
chicken & almond pilaf 134
eggplant timbale 140
herby stuffed peppers 144
honeyed rice pudding 202
Hungarian chorba 32
mushroom & thyme risotto 126
pork with black bean sauce 108
quick pilau rice 128
salmon & asparagus risotto 174
spiced date & chickpea pilaf 134
vanilla rice pudding 202
rigatoni: mushroom & tomato rigatoni 122
rillettes
chicken, pork, & prune rillettes 62
duck, pork, & apple rillettes 62
risottos
barley risotto with blue cheese 136
barley risotto with garlic & cilantro cream 136
beet & mascarpone risotto 126
mushroom & thyme risotto 126
salmon & asparagus risotto 174
romesco sauce 70
rum
hot buttered rum 230
poached apples with buttered rum 230

saffron: baked seafood with saffron 96
salads
baked mackerel with hot potato salad 78
lentil salad with sardines & peas 60
warm lentil & feta salad 60
salmon
baked salmon with basil bean mash 112
baked salmon with pesto 96
fish pie 166
fish terrine 58
mixed fish & spinach gratin 166
salmon & asparagus risotto 174
salmon & crab chowder 26
salmon avgolemono 118
salmon steaks with lemon & tarragon foam 160
salmon-wrapped cod with leeks 150
zucchini, salmon, & asparagus frittata 66
salsa: avocado & red onion salsa 158
sardines: lentil salad with sardines & peas 60
sausages
garlicky pork & sage pâté 52
sausage tagliatelle 84
turkey & sausage stew 80
see also chorizo
seafood: baked seafood with saffron 96
shrimp
baked seafood with saffron 96
Thai broth with noodles & shrimp 46
soups 16–49
butternut & orange soup 28
caramelized onion soup 42
carrot & cumin soup 34

cheesy cauliflower soup 48
cheesy pumpkin soup 48
chicken & tortelloni soup 24
chicken broth with mini herb dumplings 18
cock-a-leekie soup 38
crab gumbo 40
crab gumbo soup 162
curried vegetable & chicken soup 36
French onion soup 42
gingered carrot soup 20
haddock & bacon chowder 26
lamb & barley broth 32
leek, potato, & Stilton soup 38
minestrone soup 36
mulligatawny soup 20
old English pea & ham soup 22
pesto & lemon soup 24
salmon & crab chowder 26
spiced parsnip soup 34
split pea & parsnip soup 22
Thai broth with fish dumplings 46
Thai broth with noodles & shrimp 46
Thai coconut & butternut soup 28
tomato & red pepper soup 30
tomato, lentil, & chorizo soup 44
tomato, lentil, & eggplant soup 44
vegetable broth with dumplings 18
spaghetti: balsamic tomatoes with spaghetti 142
Spanish chicken with chorizo 86

spiced berry and pear compote 224
spinach
barley risotto with blue cheese 136
cauliflower & spinach balti 139
chicken & tortelloni soup 24
keema aloo 102
mixed fish & spinach gratin 166
spinach & egg tarka dhal 146
warm lentil & feta salad 60
spotted dick 182
squid
baked seafood with saffron 96
tomato-braised squid with chorizo 104
tomato-braised squid with red onion 104
stews
chicken & navy bean stew 86
Irish stew 72
lamb stew with dumplings 72
pepperonata & white bean stew 132
turkey & sausage stew 80
stifado 116
Stilton cheese
beef & Guinness puff pie 170
leek, potato, & Stilton soup 38
strawberries
berry compote with syllabub cream 192
strawberry cheesecake 196
sweet potatoes
barley risotto with garlic & cilantro cream 136

chicken & sweet potato balti 92
harissa baked chicken with sweet potato 92
mushroom & sweet potato balti 138
sweet & sour pork 108

tagliatelle
baked seafood with saffron 96
chicken & chorizo tagliatelle 84
Italian spiced chicken with pesto 110
sausage tagliatelle 84
tamarind paste: tamarind beef with ginger beer 164
tarka dhal 146
terrines
fish terrine 58
roasted vegetable terrine 70
smoked haddock & chive terrine 58
Thai broth with fish dumplings 46
Thai broth with noodles & shrimp 46
timbale: eggplant timbale 140
toddy: cider toddy 226
toffee sauce: mini banana & date puddings 178

tomatoes
baked eggs on toast 56
baked seafood with saffron 96
balsamic tomatoes with spaghetti 142
chicken & tortelloni soup 24
chilied corn 68
chilied beet & tomato chutney 214
crab gumbo 40
eggplants with baked eggs 130
harissa baked chicken with sweet potato 92
Italian spiced chicken with pesto 110
keema mutter 102
minestrone soup 36
Moroccan meatballs 74
mulligatawny soup 20
mushroom & tomato rigatoni 122
pepperonata 132
pesto baked tomatoes 142
romesco sauce 70
sausage tagliatelle 84
tarka dhal 146
tomato & red pepper soup 30
tomato & squash curry 128
tomato braised squid with chorizo 104

tomato, lentil, & chorizo soup 44
tomato, lentil, & eggplant soup 44
tomato-braised squid with red onion 104
vegetable goulash 124
warm lentil & feta salad 60
tortelloni: chicken & tortelloni soup 24
tortillas
cheesy bacon & rosemary tortilla 54
red pepper & chorizo tortilla 54
trout
fish terrine 58
trout spirals with lemon foam 160
turkey
Moroccan meatballs 74
turkey & cranberry meatloaf 64
turkey & cranberry puff pie 80
turkey & sausage stew 80

vanilla beans
peach compote with vanilla 192
vanilla rice pudding 202
vanilla extract
prune & vanilla fool 190
vanilla custard pots 184

venison puff pie 152
vodka: boozy berry punch 224

watercress: warm lentil & feta salad 60
whiskey
cider toddy 226
hot toddy oranges 198

zucchini
eggplant ratatouille with baked eggs 130
minestrone soup 36
roasted vegetable terrine 70
zucchini & fava bean frittata 66
zucchini, salmon, & asparagus frittata 66

acknowledgments

Executive Editor: Eleanor Maxfield
Managing Editor: Clare Churly
Deputy Art Director: Yasia Williams
Designer: Penny Stock
Photographer: Stephen Conroy
Home Economist: Sara Lewis
Props Stylist: Liz Hippisley
Senior Production Controller: Caroline Alberti

We would like to thank **Morphy Richards** for the kind loan of their slow cookers for recipe testing.

Special photography: © Octopus Publishing Group Limited/Stephen Conroy